D1009406

Express

Yourself

What others are saying...
Express

"A valuable guide to becoming a more loving and creative person. It offers simple, yet dynamic exercises to help overcome blocks to achieving your highest potential."
>—John Gray, author of *Men are from Mars, Women are from Venus* and *What You Can Feel You can Heal*

"A valuable contribution and a pleasure to read. Use it, enjoy it!"
>—Gay and Kathlyn Hendricks, authors of *Conscious Loving* and *Ten Second Miracle*

"*Express Yourself* takes you by the hand and heart and leads you through the darkness of past wounds and limiting beliefs into the loving light of understanding. If its contents were known by everyone the world would be a better place in which to live. I highly recommend it."
>—Leonard Laskow, M.D., author of *Healing With Love*

"Most of us having been taught that self criticism is virtue, think that which is most negative to be most true—that is a lie. Joy Freeman knows that what is most true is experience rather than some judgment about experience. Her book is about getting beyond judgment and contacting experience. Joy is the willingness to face feelings and become a creator."
>—Brad Blanton, author of *Radical Honesty* and *Radical Parenting*

Yourself

"A rich, informative, and inspiring road map to inner joy and a life of celebration. Joy Lynn Freeman shares her heart and wisdom in a way that will uplift you and change your life if you put these great ideas into practice."

> —Alan Cohen, author of *Dare To Be Yourself* and *The Dragon Doesn't Live Here Anymore*

"In her book *Express Yourself*, Joy Freeman provides a valuable guide for cultivating creativity and expressing wholeness. I highly recommend this work to those who are seeking the fulfillment of their soul's deeper purpose and are following the prompting of spirit in their daily lives."

> —Carolyn Anderson, co-founder of Global Family and co-author of *The Rings of Empowerment*

"A marvelous book that puts new and expanded meaning into words like discovery, fulfillment and empowerment. The discovery of inner truth and the ability to let it out are vital to fulfillment and this book will help you find them."

> —Richard Fuller, columnist, "Metaphysical Reviews"

"A unique and excellent book in which Joy Freeman courageously expresses herself from deep within her own truth. She joins the reader creatively and passionately in their path towards self-discovery and self expression. I found the exercises, personal examples and other tools she used to be particularly valuable. She makes the "path of truth" an exciting adventure."

> —Irv Katz, Ph.D., President of International University of Professional Studies

Copyright © 1999 by Joy Lynn Freeman
All rights reserved. No part of this book shall be reproduced, stored in a retrieval system, or transmitted by any means, electronic, mechanical, photocopying, recording, or otherwise without written permission from the publisher. Although every precaution has been taken in the preparation of this book, the publisher and author assume no responsibility for errors or omissions. Neither is any liability assumed for damages resulting from the use of the information contained herein.

A SoundStar Productions Publication
Printed in the United States of America on recycled paper

Editors: Jan Edelstein and Blessingway Services
Cover Art: Karen "Blu" Kroll
Cover and book design, typesetting: Paul Peterson

Publisher's Cataloging-in-Publication Data
Freeman, Joy Lynn.
Express yourself : discover your inner truth, creative self,
and the courage to let it out / by Joy Lynn Freeman. — 1st ed.
p. cm.
Preassigned LCCN: 98-090225
ISBN: 0-9623861-9-7

1. Creative ability. 2. Creation (Literary, artistic, etc.)
3. Self-realization. I. Title.

BF408.F74 1998   153.3'5
                                  QBI97-41497

10 9 8 7 6 5 4 3 2 1

Discover Your Inner Truth,
Creative Self, & the
Courage to Let It Out

Express Yourself

Joy Lynn Freeman

acknowledgments

Writing this book has been a spiritual and psychological process involving many people over many years. I want to thank a number of special individuals who have made this book possible, either by their part in my transformation or by their direct support on the technical end. Thank you to: Lisa DeLongchamps, my first personal teacher who, way ahead of the times, opened me to expanded ways of approaching life; Alan Cohen, whose heart opening approach first melted some of my barriers and inspired me to live in Maui where much of my healing occurred; Michael Stillwater for all the heart songs that reached in deeper than most anything else and began the process of opening up my voice; Gay and Kathlyn Hendricks, whose fabulous books and powerful trainings had a profound impact; the many authors and workshop leaders whose words and teachings helped transform my life; Eddy Eckley for editing and his loving support; Paul Peterson for his creative graphics work; and Jan Edelstein who selflessly offered countless hours of editing that ultimately helped transform my extensive growth path into a book I could share with others. My sincerest thank you to all of you and to Great Spirit for all the incredible blessings that have brought me to this point.

contents

PART THREE
Express Your Courageous and Creative Self

Conclusion

introduction

I have been on a journey of discovering the truths of life since I was seventeen years old. After many twists and turns and stops and starts, I have come to believe that the truths of life are inherently connected with our personal truths and these truths will continuously and ever more clearly reveal themselves when we are willing to face and honor what we find within.

At times in the past I have been attached to what I thought were the truths of life, and there were times when practically everything I had believed in lost its luster, leaving me dispirited and unmotivated. I have finally come to a place in the middle where I feel quite passionately that I know what the truth is for me and what I believe are the keys to a vital, creative, and expressive life. I no longer feel I know the answers for everyone because we are each unique and our roads to integration, happiness, and fulfillment may be different. I do, however, definitely know what has worked powerfully for me and can stand enthusiastically and firmly on this as my truth. I also believe that what has been so effective in enhancing the quality of my life can work for you as well.

This is not to say that things are always rosy in my life, but I have developed a sense of peace and willingness to be with whatever happens, and have found ways to promote and maintain aliveness, spontaneity, and fulfillment. To embark on the journey to this heightened state of living requires that we let go of much of what we have been taught, led, or programmed to believe, both consciously and unconsciously. Although this process of letting go is not always quick and easy, it is rewarding and enriching, and provides fuel for a deeper level of satisfaction than we may believe possible.

We are all creatively expressive beings and without so many of the constraints, rules and judgments that we have learned to live with, most people would begin to express their creative colorful sides in their personal lives, work, or through various art forms. This expression of creativity could also be used in service to the world. There are many different approaches and facets to living a more fulfilling expressive life, which this book will explore in great detail. But if I were to encapsulate my experience and philosophy into a few words I would say this:

> *The more we know our truth and are able to express it responsibly to ourselves and others, the more our lives begin to creatively express who we truly are, rather than some idea of what we should be.*

Our relationships take on a richer, more honest and harmonious dynamic. We begin to be appreciated for who we truly are rather than the roles we play. Our bodies function at a higher level with more constant energy. We feel a sense of creativity moving through much of what we do and our livelihood in the world becomes a joyful expression of who we are, what we believe in, and what we love to do.

You have nothing to lose by giving the ideas and exercises in this book a try—except aspects of your life you are currently dissatisfied with. Personally, my life has changed from what I call "the never satisfied syndrome"—being tired all the time, hating my work, finding fault with many things, having horrible relationships—to a life where I spend most of my time in a state of deep satisfaction and gratitude. Moreover, my life is continually transforming into a joyful creative expression of who I am and am becoming.

These are some of the possible fruits that I offer to you if you are willing to open your eyes, ears, and heart to what might be a whole new outlook on life, or a new twist on old themes. Some of what I propose in the book might sound familiar to you, either because you have already begun to explore other possibilities or because you recognize essential truths when you encounter them.

A deep felt sense of recognition is how I began the journey. It happened thirty years ago. I was seventeen years old, in college and living in an area of Miami, Florida, called Coconut Grove. My fellow students were all trying to outdo each other with fancier cars, clothes, and other possessions. I had smoked some marijuana to be socially acceptable, although when I did I would sink into depths of depression and self-deprecation. Moving out of my normal mode of existence and state of mind let me see and feel what lay beneath—despair, hopelessness, and a deeply felt sense of brutal aloneness. They were my bottom line, as they are for most us living in a world of separation from the true essence of love.

I'll never forget the night that changed my life forever. On that particular night I was guided to a yoga class that was being held at night under the moonlit, starry Miami sky, with the sounds of palm fronds blowing in the wind. The class was taught by a man who wore a turban, spoke with a thick east Indian accent, and seemed to be at peace with himself. When the class was over, the feeling of newfound freedom in my body absolutely amazed me and was enhanced by the connection with nature that I had experienced doing yoga postures under the stars. Then the teacher invited us in for a talk in which he mentioned simple, essential truths of life, and applied them to Western lifestyles. I enthusiastically affirmed everything he said, feeling as if I had found home. No doubt this was because he was telling me what deep inside I already knew to be true. I felt elated. To hear somebody speak what felt so right and real after feeling so dissatisfied with everyday life, seemed an absolute miracle. From that day on, I began reading books and taking every class I could on the subject of life. As I read, I remember feeling a sense of recognition, as if I were just being reminded of what deep inside I knew to be true.

I hope this book will be a reminder for you as well, of what you already know, either consciously or deep inside. If you have not been so fortunate as to have someone meet you there, I want to take the opportunity to be your friend and guide who takes you to a world of new possibilities, that with a little focus can literally turn your outer world completely around. It might turn it upside down at times, but I can assure you it is worth the ride. The discovery of this new world does not guarantee that you will never again feel dissatisfaction. But any sense of being a victim will be changed to a state of empowerment; feelings of fear, pain, isolation, or defensiveness in relating to others will be transformed to deeper levels of connectedness, safety, and intimacy; and feelings of boredom or resignation in daily work will give way to inspiration, creativity, and the desire to make a difference. You will also find that you have the ability to truly be of *service*—bringing your natural gifts and passions forth to the world.

I invite you to embark with me on the *path of truth*—a journey of self-discovery that will lead you to greater creativity, joy, and fulfillment. Though this path has many unknowns, you will also experience many wonderful adventures. Let this book serve as a guidebook for the journey. It is filled with information to assist you in discovering your own insights and contains countless tools to help you open to a new way of being. The tools and exercises contained within have all been tried and tested on myself and countless other individuals. Many of the exercises have been part of workshops and retreats I have led and have consistently brought about powerful results. You can do them alone, though it is helpful to meet with friends and go through them together.

Part I, "Prime Yourself for the Journey," is an overview of the way to self-discovery and change. It expresses some of the basic concepts from which to embark into more uncharted territory. Part I also provides some of the first tools that plant seeds for change and will help you create a ground of trust with yourself—an important step that prepares you for the deeper work.

Part II, "Discover Your Deeper Self," takes you farther in your inner travels, to a place where you can come face-to-face with your deeper truths. This section offers ways to more honestly answer the following questions which deepens your self-awareness; What are you feeling? What hidden or old pains are you harboring? How is the pain others are causing you a reflection of yourself? How do you operate, and what are your motives? How hard are you on yourself? What do you believe, and how is it running you? Once your deeper truths are discovered, there are many tools provided to help you release the energy blocked by old ways of being. Freeing this untapped energy will open you up to your more empowered, creative, and expressive self.

Part III, "Express Your Courageous and Creative Self," is about taking the insights and experiences of your inner truths out into the world. It focuses on creating new, more powerful behaviors and states of being. It concerns reshaping your life—how you interact with others, how you maintain yourself in the light of your discoveries and truths, what actions you choose to take, and ultimately how you serve. It is about allowing yourself the joy of creative expression.

The most exciting part of this journey is watching things unfold in ways you never dreamed possible. It is truly a marvel and a blessing to experience yourself as a creator expressing on the canvas of your life. As you accept the challenge of opening to the possibilities of a different style of living, you will be blessed with many rewards. I wish you a powerful journey.

Prime Yourself
for the Journey

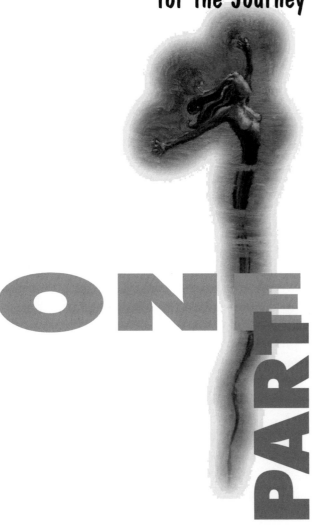

PART 1

chapter one
The Path of Truth

This book is about being able to express your true self freely and fully in all aspects of your life. Unfortunately expressing ourselves fully, whether it is in the form of telling the simple truth about our feelings, acting in opposition to society's norm, projecting ourselves boldly in the world, or standing out as different, is not often sanctioned by friends, family or society. In general people feel inhibited to express their uniqueness.

Expressing ourselves fully and honestly is something we are not trained to do. We are trained to tell half-truths and omit painful or embarrassing facts. We do this in the name of being "nice," to avoid hurting other people's feelings, or to protect ourselves from the reactions of others. In addition, we have been taught not to be "selfish." This is considered egotistical, conceited, self-centered, and negative. Consequently, to speak our truth, if our truth is in opposition to others' needs and desires, is seen as a crime, ultimately punishable by a sentence in purgatory (or so deduced by our subconscious). Even if we are fortunate enough to know what our truth is, after all the programming of what we should and shouldn't feel and do, it is a brave soul who can voice that truth.

We have also become adept at using a great variety of *personas* or masks. This term refers to styles of behavior that we employ to get attention and approval, or to cope with our particular life situations. These personas take on personality characteristics such as the caretaker, helper, nice guy, got it all together, sex pot, helpless one, rebel, independent, or provider. These roles usually become part of us either because we emulate what we observed growing up or because we decided, consciously or subconsciously, to behave a certain way to cope with traumatic or unpleasant events. Although in some ways these roles seem to help us, in actuality they can hold us back. The problem is they usually inhibit our ability to fully express who we are because we become stuck in them, like wearing a coat you can't take off. The masks we wear most often could be helpful as part of a repertoire of behaviors in the world, but when we no longer use them by choice, we lose the whole range of possibilities for how we might otherwise choose to express ourselves.

So we have a challenge. If we can't say what our truth is, because we need to fit within a certain norm to be acceptable, comfortable or appropriate, or because it has become habitual for safety or approval, then where is there room just to be ourselves? And if we could be ourselves—expressing fully, what would that be like?

In addition, I propose there is another challenge to full self-expression besides the restrictions programmed by our family and culture or adopted by ourselves. Have you ever felt frustrated, disgusted or hopeless with the way our modern culture functions? With all the apparent wealth in our society, more and more people still become homeless and destitute. Moreover, growing numbers are becoming addicted to drugs, and the suicide rate for youth is rising at an alarming rate. Even if we function within our society well enough to deal successfully with financial issues and live a semblance of a "normal" life, we may find ourselves experiencing another type of hopelessness—not out of worry about where our next meal will come from but we may despair of ever feeling truly "satisfied."

When concerned with paying for food, shelter, or other bills, it is sometimes difficult to see dissatisfaction as the core issue that it is. It is easy to say, "If I just had my basic needs met, everything would be great. Then I could relax and be happy." However, as we move beyond having our basic needs met, and start fulfilling our desires for more abundance—a better job, travel, vacations, fancier homes, better relationships, or more growth seminars—the underlying dissatisfaction becomes more obvious. Whether we live in a state of abject poverty or in comfort and acceptable complacency, the underlying craving is the same. The poorest beggar and the wealthiest person usually experience the same or similar core issues.

What is it we are all seeking? What are we all craving that has us running around like dogs chasing their tails to satisfy our endless external desires, that has us blaming our partners, children, relatives, coworkers, bosses, government, or circumstances for our woes, that has us endlessly feeding consumerism to the point of smothering and poisoning our planet, that has us killing ourselves with diseases and accidents and torturing each other with wars and human injustices. What is this "endless aching need" as Bette Midler sang in the hit song *The Rose*?

The question "What are we seeking?" is an existential one. Although I don't presume to have the definitive answer, I will venture to speculate. I believe our desire for connection to the oneness of life is the source of all our striving, whether we are conscious of it or not.

> *I propose that what we all have in common, from the pauper to the rich man, from the criminal to the man of distinction, is the desire to be connected to that which is the essence of life and to feelings of love.*

By love I do not mean transient romantic love, though we think that will provide the answer, because aspects of it feel close to what we are truly searching for. Instead I am referring to essential, unconditional love that seems to be only found "from whence we came and to where we are going"—a connection to the very essence of life itself.

Many people say that such a connection is only possible when we die. Does the only hope lie in death, then? Can the only solution to this worldly life of painful separation from the source of all love, peace, and harmony be to live lives of desperation or complacency, biding our time until we can "go home" again—home to that place where we can fully experience those feelings of connectedness, peace, warmth, and ultimate love that we hear about from people who have had near-death experiences? Is that why so many people live lives of slow death, through abusive habits or illness—in order to get home faster? Is that why so many individuals obliterate their feelings through drugs, alcohol, or other addictions just to forget everything until they can finally return to the source? Is living our lives in perpetual avoidance of this pain of separation the only tactic? Are there other viable options?

I propose that there is another way, although it may not be easy. Learning anything new, especially for which we have no experience and few role models can be challenging. But if you open your mind and heart to the possibilities of this new way, however it contradicts premises and concepts you presently hold, a new way of life can be found. I do not promise that this new way forever frees us from the pain and challenges of living this life of separation that prevails here on planet earth. But this new way can make moments of feeling "connectedness" more frequent and open us to experiencing other human beings from a new perspective. Feelings of separation from oneself, others, or life, will give way to a growing feeling of being connected, a willingness to be here, and the ability to fully express ourselves and participate in life. We can get a clearer sense of who we are and what unique things we have to offer that feel right to the core of our being. We might even find that we are spending more of our lives in a state of satisfaction and deeply-felt gratitude rather than continual dissatisfaction. We might find that we don't have to waste so much energy insulating ourselves from our deeper truth and the reaction of the outer world to that truth. This would make much more energy available to maintain vibrant health, achieve abundance, and joyfully creatively express ourselves. And such moments of losing ourselves in the act of creative expression could be some of our greatest moments of feeling the connection to timelessness, to the essence of life.

I call this journey the *path of truth*. The destination of the journey is not a static goal, rather the journey is an ever-evolving, ongoing process where the environment and the scenery begin to take on more and more of the qualities mentioned above as the travel continues.

The road to a life that fully and freely expresses more of who we truly are starts with our own daily personal expression of who we are. We do that by telling the truth to ourselves about what is real for us, what we are feeling, and what has meaning for us. Then we become willing to take the risks involved in letting that truth be known. This is not something that one learns to do overnight. It is an art, and like learning any art form, it takes time, practice, and patience. Much of this book will address this subtle art of being fully in our truth. Once we have learned this skill, we have created an optimal environment that allows our creative selves to fully blossom.

I call this process the path of truth because the concept of truth comes up many times as a critical element to creating a life that expresses who we are. Much of the journey is about gaining ever-increasing knowledge of our personal truths and learning to know, accept and express ourselves and such truths more fully.

But what is truth? To say something is the truth seems to exclude other options, opinions, or beliefs. There are universally accepted truths like gravity and other physical laws; and there are philosophical truths, of which there are many differences of opinion. Although the truth is that which cannot be disputed, almost everything can be disputed. How often do we hear that there has been a new scientific discovery that contradicts something we previously held to be the absolute truth. How many religions claim to protect the only truth. However, one distinguishing characteristic of the path of truth is that there are no absolute truths, and at the same time there is only one truth—your truth.

The only truth is that which is true for you and that cannot be disputed by another. What filters through your set of life experiences, circumstances, lessons, and being is unique only to you, and can only be seen and felt by you. This means that *the* truth can only be *your* truth.

Henry Palmer, creator of *Avatar Training*, adds another dimension to the definition of the truth. He says that truth is when your beliefs align with your experience. You can have an idea that something seems true, but when your personal experience supports your beliefs then to you it is a truth. For example, for a person who grew up in a ghetto, truth may be that the world is not a safe place, while a person who grew up in a more loving environment would not hold this truth. Though personal truths can be changed with new experiences, healing work, and reprogramming, unless someone is willing to do the work necessary to change their truth, it will persist, continuing to be substantiated by their experience.

Although you may meet others who share some of your truths, your own truth will never exactly match someone else's. The sad thing is that wars are fought over trying to change people's truths or trying to make them uniform. Such attempts are fruitless and absurd since no two individuals—with their beliefs, experiences, and inherent makeup—are the same.

> *With society's attempts to congeal many truths into only a few, we as individuals have lost touch with our own unique truth.*

Although we all have opinions and ideas that seem to be our own and different from what society dictates, very few of us actually live in the ever-flowing, exceedingly dynamic truth of the moment. In other words, we have lost touch with what is real for us on the deepest level, to the point that most of us don't even know how to begin to access that deeper truth. We are so programmed with ideas about what is believed to be true, or what should or shouldn't be done, said, or felt, that there is very little room for what is. However, with the notion of "what is," we can begin to bridge our personal truths with the universal truth. In more esoteric terms, universal truth can be described as the never-changing in the midst of the ever-changing, or the only truth in the midst of the many truths which equates to our deeper or higher knowing.

The journey of the path of truth is to come to the only one truth there is—your truth and your own experience of reality. Though absolute as that truth may be for you, it will often differ from other's. Therefore, you must be willing to give up attachment to the idea that your's is the only right truth. Giving up attachment to this does not mean replacing your truth with someone else's; it means letting go of the notion of convincing others to accept your's as their own. Much of our energy and creative juices are wasted trying to get others to take on our truths. The key is to learn to let others have their truth while you have yours, regardless of the price you may have to pay, such as disapproval, emotional upsets, or threats of abandonment.

Although the path of truth may not be always easy, the rewards are great.

> *The key to the path is in the knowing—knowing what our truth is at such an essential level that we can distinguish it from the many voices within our head as well as from the many other voices coming at us from without.*

When we know our truth so that it stands out above the rest of the chorus, we can hold firm and take whatever actions or inactions are necessary based on that truth. Being clear about our truth gives us a foundation of inner knowing that provides strength to face the challenges that arise in life. I call participating on this journey being a spiritual adventurer. The spiritual adventurer knows how to surrender to the flow, armed only with a garment of truth and connection to the source of that truth. This way of living is synonymous with living in integrity and has us commit our lives to the truth on every level. This degree of integrity raises our self esteem which in turn has us believe in our deservability—that we deserve to be loved and succeed at what we desire.

A question often asked is how can we tell the difference between our real truth (our higher or deeper knowing) and what only appears to be the truth (that which arises from ego or fear)? Typically, our deeper knowing speaks in a whisper through our subtle senses, such as through vague feelings, body sensations, intuition, or gentle thoughts in the back of our minds. By contrast thoughts based on fear usually speak as strong words we hear in our head and are associated with "shoulds." Discerning the difference between these voices is a fine art and many of the practices and tools described in this book are geared toward learning to know the difference and to knowing your personal truth in any given moment. These practices heighten sensitivity to the subtle messages that help you discern the difference. Like any art, the ability to make such distinctions must be practiced before it is truly mastered. As mastery at knowing and the courage to stand on one's personal truth is gained, life becomes richer, more vibrant, and more profoundly connected to all that is.

I have watched myself move from a life of contraction, drama, unhealthy and unhappy relationships, low energy, inner tension, and general dissatisfaction to a place of overflowing abundance, joy, gratitude and creativity. The quality of every aspect of my life has improved significantly, and will continue to do so as I continue to do the "work." The work I refer to is not dull or arduous as we have come to associate with the word but instead colorful, engaging, sometimes amusing, and other times challenging. Because upleveling our lives does take some energy and focus, one of the keys to this path is an overriding sense of dedication and willingness to creating positive change.

As with any new endeavor, getting started often takes a concerted effort, and extra focus is required to develop momentum. Even more challenging may be reversing a downward spiral to begin movement in a new direction. However, let me assure you, once the wheel has begun to turn in the direction you want to go, there is an upward spiraling effect making it progressively easier to keep moving in the new direction.

This book contains many tools and practices that function as stepping stones on the path; which ones you choose, and in what order, is your choice. What is essential is that you make the commitment to begin the journey and commit to sticking with whatever practices or tools you choose for at a least a month at a time. Many of the practices may become an integral part of your life that you will use for years to come. As you begin experiencing the positive results of working with these tools, you will be motivated and inspired to continue.

I caution you, however, not to take on too much initially. The tendency at the beginning of any self-improvement program, whether geared toward exercise, diet, or personal growth, is to become overzealous and to attempt more than you can handle. Since this is a path of truth, which means knowing and following your inner truth, you must honor your pace and be honest and realistic about how much you can do right now. One new practice done consistently is worth far more than multiple efforts done sporadically then ultimately dropped. Take small bites and chew slowly.

On this path, I have studied with many teachers and taken numerous workshops. Over the years I have spoken to other students who had not benefited as much from these classes while I had gotten so much out of the teaching or workshop. What made the difference, I realized, was that I would do "the homework." Whether the teachers gave us specific assignments or not, I would always select practices or exercises I could do regularly. I would make time for the work, no matter how busy my life seemed to be, because I knew my life depended on it.

Consequently, I want to stress the importance of putting into practice some of what you read, whether it is an actual exercise or just heightening your awareness. Some of the tools don't take time, only a focusing of attention because they involve listening to or watching certain words, actions, or behaviors. It is possible to commit to some degree of practice no matter what your life circumstances are. Having a friend or friends, "path partners" to discuss things or do the exercises with can be very helpful.

Although the path of truth is highly rewarding, it can be challenging as well. Once you start shaking things up and shining the light of awareness on previously hidden places, you may feel worse for a while. Know that this is part of a natural healing process just as a fever burns out microorganisms from the body, or a boil must erupt and drain before it smooths over. Understand that the difficult circumstances or feelings are temporary and will pass. They become your passport to higher ground.

There may also be plateaus along the way where you think you are stuck and haven't made any progress. However, at such times, even though things may feel the same as they were before you started, once you have made positive movement or an internal shift, you are further along the road and never really go back to where you started. It's like spiraling up a mountain. As you circle around to a similar area on the mountain, the view may be essentially the same, but you are now higher up. In time circumstances will improve.

Even though we are on a path and will pass by many different destinations along the way, remember that this is a never-ending journey. Let the joys and sorrows along the way be the destination. Let what you hold onto be only what you have learned and even be willing to let go of that if necessary.

For the path of truth is a path to freedom. In becoming free, we become light. To become free, it is necessary to let go of what is not possible to hold onto anyway—restrictions and dictates of the mind as well as the seriousness and struggle of life. As we let go, little by little, not demanding more of ourselves than we are ready for, we begin to taste freedom—freedom to know and express who we are, freedom to create what is true for us, freedom to love, and freedom to be of service in a meaningful way. Let us begin the journey on the path of truth.

chapter TWO

The Six Steps of Personal Change—

An Overview of the Journey

The path of truth is a journey of change—change that creates fertile ground for the seeds of our creativity, expression, joy, and fulfillment. This change most effectively takes place in six steps. It can occur without going through all the steps, though my experience has shown that when steps are left out, the change can take longer or be incomplete. Sometimes a step may only be touched on lightly, but any level of incorporation is more effective than none at all. Each of these steps will often merge with the next, though sometimes the order varies. This chapter will outline the flow that generally occurs.

In Part II and III we will go into much more detail on many of the subjects touched upon here, illustrating them with further stories and examples. If a topic seems foreign or incomplete, know that it will be addressed more fully as you read on. Since the process of change can feel very amorphous and sometimes confusing, this chapter is meant to give you a helpful framework. In the workshops I have led I have seen that when the logical mind understands what is about to occur, it allows other parts of ourselves to open up.

I consider the path of truth a *psychospiritual* process. It is an integration of the journey of psychoemotional healing and a spiritual way of life. The intention of the clearing and balancing that occurs through the steps taken in the process of change is not only to open our creative, expressive selves, and to experience a more fulfilling life, it is also to foster a deeper connection to our understanding of the Divine.

Willingness

The first step to creating change is *willingness*. Willingness means you have a strong desire and intention to have an aspect of your life be different than it is. Change requires a certain amount of energy output—the amount necessary to change a spiral of energy from one direction to another—and this, in turn, necessitates dedication. We often must reach a place of exasperation or crisis before we become willing to go through whatever is necessary to make this change. In studies on human nature, it has been found that we are more motivated by moving away from pain than moving toward pleasure. Consequently, in order to be fully committed to doing whatever it takes to make a change, we must reach a place where we can honestly say the pain, or dissatisfaction of letting things continue the way they are is greater than the effort or discomfort involved in making the change.

If you are not at such a place already, then think about an aspect of your life that you currently find greatly unfulfilling, frustrating, or painful. If just the thought of it is not enough to access your willingness, then close your eyes and imagine how your life would be one year from now, five years, ten, twenty, or more, if you didn't make a change in that particular area. Try to feel how awful it would be to experience the cumulative effect of being stuck over time. When you let go of believing your life would be better if only someone close to you would change, someone new would show up, or your doctor or therapist could fix things, then you are on your way to true willingness.

> *You have true willingness—the kind that can create a miracle—when you can honestly say, "I am ready to change. I know it is only me who can make the change, and I am willing to do whatever it takes."*

When I do transformational work with clients, I always begin a session by ascertaining their level of willingness. At times when I have forgotten to do this or did not think it was necessary, invariably, we would come to a place where there was strong resistance to forward movement. Then I would remember this point and go back to access their willingness. Just the client's expression of willingness would often be all that was necessary. If they discovered they weren't really willing, because they thought changing something could only be done at too high a price, then it became clear that this was not the time to work on that issue.

Once you have acknowledged that you are truly willing to change, the use of *affirmative questions* can be helpful. These are questions that serve as an active way of saying affirmations. I ask myself, my higher self, Spirit, or any other energy source that may be instrumental in my process: "What must I see, know, feel, or do in order to... (the desired goal or change)?" It may be an inner change, such as strength or the ability to surrender; or it may be an outer manifestation. What I am doing is changing a positive statement about what I want (an affirmation) and turning it into a question. This lets all the forces at work know that I am truly willing to do my part rather than just asking for it to be magically bestowed upon me. Though universal forces and divine grace can and do play a part in personal transformation, generally we must meet spirit halfway and do our part as well. This question/prayer is a strong statement of your intention to participate in the change. Although expressing your willingness as statement, affirmative question, or prayer helps the process, it is most important that you find the place deep within you that is open and willing to see, feel, or do whatever is necessary to create the desired change. (See Chapter 13 for more about this topic.)

Awareness

Once willingness for change and the dedication to do whatever it takes is firmly established, the next step is to cultivate *awareness* and insight. Awareness is the subtle art of paying attention to what we do and say with the intention of exposing to ourselves what is and isn't working. We begin to become aware of what we are doing that no longer serves us. With the willingness to know the truth and keeping an open heart and mind, it is truly amazing the things you will begin to notice. In various circumstances just asking yourself the question, "What is the truth here?" will greatly assist this process. Such awareness may also be stimulated by ideas in a book, other people's experiences, workshops, or spontaneous flashes of insight. However, this initial awareness is only effective if we extend it into our daily lives, watching for patterns of behavior, words or tone of voice that we use to talk to ourselves or others and any other habits that do not fully serve us. Awareness can also be enhanced through the practice of meditation and stilling of the mind.

A natural progression of awareness and insight is what is called *owning*. Owning requires coming to a place of the deepest honesty within yourself and acknowledging that a trait, behavior, or quality actually exists in you. No matter how much we have come to believe the opposite, a great moment of truth and readiness to move on occurs when we accept and own aspects of ourselves and our behaviors. For example we might come to the realization that the anger that I say "he" is filled with, is really there in me; or I truly am a sensual, sexual woman; I am an aggressive individual; I do have a self-serving, self-centered side to me. Although it may be disheartening at first, every time we uncover a new insight into our previously hidden behaviors or feelings there is a new opportunity for major shifts on many levels. This process of uncovering and owning *aspects* of ourselves—traits, feelings or behavior patterns—that we were not aware of before, be they positive or negative, is called shadow work. (See Chapter 7 for further discussion of this process.)

Being With

After we become aware of and can own a previously hidden trait or feeling, it is time to practice *being with*. Being with means allowing the emotion, behavior, or trait to just be there without judging it as wrong or bad and without having to immediately fix or eliminate it. Often when we have first owned something we do not like, we tend to judge or blame ourselves. Owning one's dark corners, negative patterns of behavior or feelings is a powerful experience in the transformation process because it not only provides a doorway to change, but also affords a prime opportunity to practice unconditionally loving ourselves—an act of fully accepting ourselves. Such a strong act of love helps restore the bond of love and trust within our inner being.

This practice of loving ourselves completely even with negative qualities or feelings, and then creating the space and time to let them be, is the practice of being with. It is the next level of owning.

The process works like this: first the light of our awareness is brought to an aspect. Then we say, "Yes, this is true—I own it." Then we let it be, without immediately trying to judge or change it—the "being with" phase. This might be letting ourselves deeply feel an emotion without resistance or noticing a destructive behavior and curtailing the internal judgment about it. Or it might be just sitting still when a feeling is welling up, rather than engaging in ways to avoid it such as eating, busyness, drugs/alcohol, or blaming. Being with is a rich process that allows the awarenesses to take hold in our consciousness so that they can no longer be denied on any level. A powerful exercise that encourages and assists being with can be found in Chapter 9.

Release

The next step is *release*—a type of expressing that entails letting go. Sometimes release happens simultaneously with the process of being with if you are fully with your feelings. Release can be as simple as making a strong statement affirming the release of a particular belief or a forceful exhalation of breath while thinking about what you want to release. The more you bring your whole body, voice, breath, and emotions into the release, the more impact it will have on your subconscious and consequently the more effective it will be. Many psychoimmunologists state that our beliefs about life and unexpressed emotions are chemically and vibrationally anchored in the cells of our bodies. What we are releasing is the cellular energetic holding pattern of an emotion, belief, or both. (See Chapter 5 for more about cellular anchoring and Chapter 10 for more about beliefs.)

Sometimes expressing a truth to someone can be a release. Other times the energetic holding is older or deeper and requires more full-bodied expression. In its fullest expression, release will take the form of crying, deep continuous or forceful breathing, shaking, hitting pillows, or freely moving the body and letting out any variety of sounds such as screaming, yelling, or moaning. (See Chapter 9 for more detail on different possibilities for release.)

Whether dealing with current day-to-day issues and emotions or clearing out old limiting patterns, when you gain awareness of your feelings and behaviors, be with them, then express and release them, you become open and ready for the next step—transformation.

Transformation

Transformation involves making new choices and decisions about what beliefs we want to hold, how we will live our lives, what we want to create, and what actions we are willing to take to bring this about. Transformation can begin by simply choosing to hold a new empowering belief or way of being instead of the old limiting pattern. We may anchor this new decision more deeply with affirmations, subliminal tapes, hypnosis, visualization, or other techniques. All of these are rendered much more effective after the being with and release phases are completed. (See Chapter 10.)

Behavior Change

Change starts with awareness of the new desired way of being, feeling, or acting. Unfortunately, too many people stop here. Actual transformative change does not become a reality until the last step is accomplished—*behavior change*. This is where we take all our new internal awarenesses and do something about them. Without behavior change, you have nothing but in-depth analysis. Some people cynically refer to this as "analysis paralysis" because after years spent discovering why their life is a certain way, no change has occurred. Learning the hows and whys of where we are today is important and helpful on this journey, but without putting what you have learned about yourself into positive practice, you will not get very far. Harville Hendrix, in *Keeping the Love You Find,* puts it very well:

> In order for changes to occur, insight must be translated into action. Whatever is created by experience must be corrected by experience, rather than mere analysis. In order to integrate our insights, we have to put ourselves in new situations and learn and practice new behaviors, which, over time and through repetition, actually change our past behaviors and beliefs.[1]

Behavior change may entail standing up for your truth, setting boundaries, or doing many things in contrast to your usual inclinations, which can take strength and self-discipline. The more you practice this the more it builds courage, not only to continue with this but to be able to reach out into the world in new and more expressive ways. (See Chapters 13 and 14 for more on this.)

The willingness to do things that are outside of your *comfort zone*—things you are not used to, that don't necessarily come easy—is essential for the change process to be complete. Don't be like many people who stop short with changing behavior. Should you find making a change difficult, daily prayers and asking for the wisdom, insight, and strength can help the process tremendously.

One of the advantages of doing the "work" and going through the other steps first is that when you get to the step of behavior change, you're so ready for the change that it doesn't require the same amount of effort and internal self-discipline as it would if you were to willfully try to change without having prepared the ground first. For example, I knew a man who harbored a lot of anger. He was very quick to respond with sharp, loud vocal attacks whenever he felt threatened emotionally or when things were not going his way and seemed out of his control. He knew this was a problem but was unwilling to do the deeper work. He felt strongly that he could simply control his behavior, but his attempts to do so were ineffective and cost him a career opportunity. Even though he managed to control his outbursts in the professional setting, he lost his job because his employer felt that he was steaming under the surface. He was able to change his outer behavior but the underlying truth of anger was "oozing out of his pores."

Conversely, one of our regular workshop participants excitedly shared with us, "I smoked pot and drank beer everyday for twenty seven years. Something happened to me yesterday (after a powerful healing experience), and I woke up today feeling that this behavior no longer serves me, and I don't want to do it anymore." As of this writing, five years have passed, and he has maintained his clean lifestyle and made other improvements in his life. He says that although he had quit for periods in the past, it was always a struggle against his desire. This time it just felt naturally right. Behavior changes made after deeper issues are exposed and the energy has been released are much easier to institute and maintain.

When we move from willingness to awareness, to being with, and ultimately to changed behaviors, our lives will reflect the completed inner change. Regardless of mistakes, mishaps, or backslides that may occur along the way, we can give ourselves acknowledgment for how much we are learning and for embarking on this challenging yet magical journey.

chapter three

Finding Peace in the Unknown and Letting Go of Struggle—
The Place Where Creativity Is Born

I was sitting on a deck overlooking a tropical jungle of lush green trees, rugged coastline, and the bluest ocean I had ever seen. I wanted to write about surrender and being in the unknown, that space from which creativity is born. I wanted to convey the power and peace of mind that occurs with the ability to surrender and embrace the unknown. Unfortunately, as had happened many other times when I sat down to write on the subject, I drew a blank.

Then something occurred that made this day feel different. I went to the cliff over the ocean and began toning and singing with my eyes closed. After a few minutes I opened my eyes, and before me was a huge school of dolphins playing and swimming. They were in pods of approximately eight each, and there were ten or more pods! They stayed near the surface and kept hovering around the area as if they were trying to hear me. When I finally stopped singing, they left. I then returned to my deck to write, feeling surely this would be the day I would tap into the stream of consciousness about the unknown. Then the words began coming through.

Being in the unknown is like that. It requires that we be patient and trust things will come when they come. Situations, people, or answers come when the time is right. They cannot be forced. If they are, the price we pay is stress and struggle. I had really wanted to begin writing the night before my dolphin experience since I was tired of waiting. I said this is it, here I go and wrote a paragraph, but I knew I was forcing it. I had to stop, as much as my will wanted to make something happen. I knew that whatever I would write in that state would be contrived and lack the spontaneity and aliveness of being born from a truly creative moment. In addition, the process would be work, drudging up the words rather than letting them flow easily. I decided to wait for them, hence when the time was right I naturally became inspired, my mind overflowing with ideas.

This has been my experience with many things. Sometimes I have let myself be in the unknown regarding aspects of my life for long periods, even a year or more, other times for only a month, a week, or a day. Being in the unknown is about a willingness to wait for the flow, to trust the process and be patient for an opening, an invitation, a sense of rightness and ease.

Trusting the process comes up when making decisions. Often we will need to wait for more information to come through, more pieces of the puzzle to show up, or simply a sense of knowing that this is the right time and choice. A good motto I use for this waiting period is "I'll know when I know." The more I trust this motto and see that when I wait for the inner knowing, as opposed to impatiently making things happen now, the more I am met by grace and ease.

The more we practice trusting and surrender, the more the inner struggle and any sense of anxiety and fear deep within dissipates. Much of the efforting in life begins to fall away and things start to flow more gently. The more we test our trust on each challenge the easier it becomes to let go. There are a number of components to support this movement toward less struggle and greater ease. Although they overlap, I will address each one separately.

Embracing Surrender

Surrender has two components. The first is a willingness to not know the answers right away—*being in the unknown*. The second is a willingness to give up preconceived outcomes—*letting go of control*.

Embracing all aspects of surrender and incorporating them into your life is one of the most difficult tasks of the journey—and holds the greatest potential for freedom. This skill allows for our greatest connection to a divine presence, as well as our greatest sense of joy, ease, flow, creativity, expression, and true place of service in the world. Surrender is a difficult yet easy and complex yet simple art. It is subtle and incorporates many paradoxes. I used to say to myself "how do I do not doing?" The answer is, you don't. It's not something you just do, yet if you sit back and do nothing—that is, do what you've always done—that doesn't work either. It cannot be learned in an academic fashion. Although intellectual understanding is helpful, mastery of this fine art comes from a deep knowing acquired through consistent practice.

This realm embraces paradox and the unknown, things difficult for the linear, logical mind. The linear mind can often get in the way of learning the art of surrender because often what we are required to do challenges the logical point of view. From the perspective of feeling and heartfelt knowing, however, it makes all the sense in the world. For it is here in the middle ground, between black and white, this choice and that choice, that miracles are born. Here one can experience ease, peace, and deep rest.

However, since we have come to attach so much value to things of the known world, we do not have training or role models for surrendering in this unknown space. Our reactions are based on fear of the unknown. Often there exist beneath our conscious awareness, feelings of emptiness, worthlessness, or loneliness. It is our willingness to be in touch with these feelings that allows us to step into the world of the unknown and surrender—that place where our connection to all of life resides. In addition, practicing the other skills and arts in this book greatly enhances the ability to surrender and be in the great unknown.

Being in the Unknown

In his book *The Path to Love*, Deepak Chopra *describes being in the unknown:*

> Reality is always on the move, shifting the known out from under us and bringing the unknown into view. Dying to the known brings knowledge that cannot be acquired any other way. The scriptures have called this "dying unto death."[2]

When you let yourself be in the unknown, you are faced with the uncomfortable feelings often associated with not having answers right away. You are also faced with another kind of unknown—leaving your world of perceived safety and security behind. No matter how much pain or dissatisfaction your current reality may cause you, it is a known and therefore appears desirable because it feels secure. But life based on this type of security becomes a prison. Even though a maximum-security prison provides the basic needs for prisoners—food and shelter—it also represents the ultimate loss of freedom. Similarly, when our inner being tells us to let go of something or attempt something new, but we choose what appears to be security over the unknown, we give up our freedom and the ability to lead truly creative, fulfilling lives.

The ability to be comfortable with not knowing can be cultivated. You can begin by not coming up with solutions or answers to your own questions or challenges right away. Instead, wait in the unknown, giving new possibilities time to surface. Do the same thing with friends who share their problems. Instead of jumping in with solutions, just listen and be supportive. You can do this by feeding back what you sense they are feeling about a situation, with no attempt to solve the problem. For example, if a friend tells you she just lost her job and at the same time her car broke down and fixing it used up her cash reserves, instead of offering a plan to deal with the situation or telling your friend how she should feel, simply listen to the details and empathize. Reflect it back, saying "I imagine you must be feeling pretty scared right now." This often has the magical effect of helping the person feel better. Trying to offer a solution to the problem—playing "Dr. Fix-it"—often leaves the individual feeling more frustrated. Part of not offering solutions is coming to terms with your own feelings about just letting something be, without trying to solve or fix it. Our inability to fix a friend's problems often taps into our own feelings of helplessness, but letting ourselves just be in this unknown place of our feelings and theirs is a step toward being able to be in the unknown.

Holding this non-fix-it attitude is a great way to be with yourself during times of challenges, questions, or decisions. Ironically, looking for immediate solutions or ruminating about the pros and cons of a possible choice will keep the answers from emerging. Answers usually become evident as an inner knowing that you cannot access if all your energy is focused on thinking and worrying. Let yourself acknowledge what you are feeling in response to a situation and give yourself the time and space to allow those feelings expression. It helps to ask yourself, "What am I feeling?" The feeling place is directly related to the unknown and is a source for our creativity.

Being in the unknown requires letting go of knowing answers, surrendering to feelings or emotions, relinquishing ideas of security, what seems like the "right" thing to do, or trying to fix problems. When we allow ourselves to be in the unknown, problems will work themselves out over time, or unforeseen solutions will arise. Although being in the unknown and letting go is not always easy to do, once these abilities are acquired they allow life to flow with much more ease and grace.

Listening and Silence

The practices of *Listening* and *silence* help us open to the unknown and creative places in life. They cultivate receptivity within us.

> *When we change our outgoing energies into a state of receptivity, we create an openness that invites something new, creative, or unexpected to occur.*

The more we can be with emptiness and open spaces in our mind and the more we get used to not always speaking the answer or the thought, the more comfortable we will be with the uncertainties of waiting for the unknown to reveal itself. Silence also promotes a state of inner peace and a sense of internal relaxation.

Try these practices to help cultivate your ability to listen and be silent. Notice if you spend a lot of time conversing, whether related to business, homemaking or just talking to friends. If this is the case, as it is for many of us, set aside time daily or at least weekly for being alone. If that seems impossible, at least make an agreement with the people in your life that you will be silent for a certain period and that they should not expect words from you during that time. It could be a day, an afternoon, an hour, or only 15 minutes. Just let it be focused time. Also notice if in conversations you spend a lot of the time being the talker. If so, practice spending more time as the listener.

It is also useful to learn a meditation technique. When starting, meditate for only five minutes a day. The key to adding any positive practice to your life is to spend a minimal amount of time doing the new activity at first so that your resistance to it will be lessened. Once you establish it as a habit, you can do it for longer periods.

Being Present

Being present refers to a state where we are just there, without judgment, without thinking of the future or the past. When we are fully in the present, we are in our senses, perhaps noticing our breathing, a breeze on our skin, an emotion, a bird chirp, or a passing cloud, while suspending judgment about it. It is a state of witnessing.

We can practice being present during our normal day. It only takes attention and focus. Much of what closes us down to the present moment is our judgment about what the moment presents to us.

> *Much of our strife and unhappiness can be traced to this: when our reality conflicts with our concept of how reality "should" be, according to our set of rules and opinions, dis-ease begins.*

When we are being present, we are in a state of complete acceptance. We allow what is to just be, with no judgments. What I mean by no judgment is letting go of our attachments to things as good or bad. It may be unrealistic to think that we can be present with everything that occurs and have no ideas or opinions about it. But practicing this as much as possible has tangible results. The Buddhists say that all suffering comes from attachments or aversions. Being in the moment involves freeing ourselves of all judgment—not only about other people but especially about ourselves and what we see as "right" and "wrong" in any situation. Being fully present with someone means letting go of our agenda for the future, upsets about the past, judgments of who they are, thoughts of what you are going to say, and anything else that takes your mind away from where you are. Even if you only do this for a few minutes, seeing people as they are in the present creates a high level of intimacy that can have a profound effect.

In working with people to help tap their creative expression, I use singing and theater improvisation. These tools require letting go to the moment for the magic to happen. When people are fully present in the manner that I have described, it is amazing to watch their creative brilliance emerge. Simply being able to be in the unknown, open space of the present moment, for even a few seconds, without thought or prejudgment, allows the impulse for something new and creative to arise. This practice can be applied to anything we do in life and especially to accessing our creativity.

Being Verses Doing

Our culture places great emphasis on action, production, and results which gives us many incredible products and comforts. Mental health and peace of mind, however, are at an all time low. This is demonstrated by the escalating suicide rate, mental illness and drug abuse. We have lost the importance of our simple "beingness;" instead our self-esteem is tied up with who we are in the eyes of the world. The message we receive from family and society is that our simple beingness is not enough. We feel we must prove ourselves, earning the right to exist. When we are brave enough to slow down and let ourselves be human "beings" instead of human "doings," a powerful transformation occurs.

I worked with a woman named Jennifer who could never maintain a relationship and was intensely dissatisfied with her career. She had considerable inner anxiety, though it was not immediately apparent since she did a good job of hiding it from herself and others. In fact, she came across as quite "together," except that she was always busy rushing around and claimed there was too much to do but never enough time to get it all done. After we worked together for a while and she let herself feel some of the deeper feelings she had been running from, she decided to arrange a sabbatical from work. She gave herself time to do nothing. Much of her identity had been tied up in what she did or produced. So as a practice to let go of her attachment to this, whenever people asked what she was doing, she said, "nothing." She became willing to be seen by people as her *authentic* self, without the cloak of her roles or accomplishments. In the initial period of just being, many emotions and issues began to surface. Her tendency had been to escape into her old addiction of "do-aholism," but as she was able to be with her feelings, they passed and a deeper level of peace and self-acceptance took their place.

It is very common for people to become over "identified" with what they do for a living, knowledge they have, or roles they play. When you take away those identities, deeper feelings such as anger, helplessness, fear, or other insecurities arise. Making space for these feelings to be there, without judgement, is a powerful practice which softens the controlling effect they can have on your life. These feelings may resurface now and then but you no longer waste so much energy trying to hide from them or pretending they do not exist with compensatory behaviors. This allows you to live life as your authentic self.

To make this shift from "doing" to "being" does not always require that we stop participating in every thing. Simply giving ourselves some empty time and space opens the door for something new to come in. However, when we desire to make a large shift in our lives, sometimes we need to completely unwind from the current existence to allow new perspectives. Even though taking time out of your normal life can be a scary proposition, if something inside you is guiding you in that direction it is worth facing that fear. Working with the many tools and exercises provided in this book can help you prepare the way to take that step.

As a recovering "do-aholic" myself, it was essential to allow long periods of not identifying with any purpose or productivity. In doing so, I faced what motivated me, including my belief systems, programs, and feelings of guilt. I saw how my sense of value as a human being was tied up in how "productive" I was. I was often motivated to do things, I realized, by ego, pride, or a desire to conceal my insecurity. Moreover, I experienced on a feeling level how so much of the intensity with which I worked was based on fear. I feared that there wouldn't be enough money to cover my basic needs along with fear that I wasn't worth anything if I didn't produce.

Although awareness of a pattern can begin to defuse it, modifying behavior really solidifies the change. Even though I was aware of why I was such a "doer," in order to truly counterbalance this habit, I had to consciously "undo" for awhile. I approached this task with an intention to face my feelings and issues, allow for stillness, and just to be. This was different from the breaks in my routine that had occurred in the past as result of burnout. In those cases I worked intensely, became exhausted, took long breaks, then started working all over again. Breaks at those times did not change my pattern since there was either exhaustion or still a lot of "busyness" connected with them.

After allowing myself the time and space to be with my feelings, learning to surrender more, and letting go of numerous identities that were not really me, I now feel my productivity springing from an entirely different motivation. All these changes mean I no longer feel anxiety when I work and, in fact, feel peaceful. I am willing to work toward goals again, and this focus is balanced by a sense of surrender, trust, and ease.

Victor Frank says in his book *Man's Search for Meaning*:

> Don't aim at success. The more you aim at it and make it a target the more you are going to miss it. For success, like happiness, cannot be pursued; it must ensue, and only does so as the unintended side effect of one's personal dedication to a cause greater than oneself or as the by-product of one's surrender to something other than oneself. Happiness must happen by not caring about it....Success will follow you precisely because you had forgotten to think of it.[3]

His statement makes the point that the more you strive to produce solely for the sake of results, the more you miss the mark. The more you can just be and enjoy the process of life rather than strive so hard for a certain outcome, the greater your chance will be of achieving the results you seek and experiencing happiness along the way.

I am not suggesting that you don't set goals or have desire for things you want in life. It is important to steer the direction of your life, just as you drive a car, otherwise the car of life will drive itself (right into a wall!). By all means set a direction, but then let it go. Balance your doing with being and see where life takes you. Something may emerge that you can't imagine at this time— something that expresses who you are even more than what you had been striving for.

Letting Go of Control

Letting go of control includes letting go of expected outcomes. You know you are attached to an outcome when you have a sense of urgency or tension about things turning out a certain way. For a moment consider this: how do you react when things do not happen the way you want them to or the flow of your life is interrupted with unexpected change? Notice how you react when others don't respond to you as you would like them to or don't do what you think they should. Think about monetary or material loss. When these things occur what emotions emerge? What do you feel in your body—tightness in your chest, a churning in your belly? What you feel is an indication of how "in control" you are trying to be. Different circumstances trigger different reactions in various people. For some, issues of money may have more potential for upset; for others, the inability to elicit a certain behavior or emotional response from someone may cause anxiety; for others, issues of organization are very important.

The *controller* is that part of us or aspect of our behavior that responds to external circumstances or internal feelings by attempting to control them. All this controlling is futile and a great waste of creative life force because feelings, other individuals, and life in general are impossible to control. The more we try, the farther we stray from our essence. We can guide the direction we want it to go, but actually control it we cannot do.

There are keys to help you notice when you are trying to be "in control," whether it is in response to something particular or just as a general modus operandi. Look for these clues in your body: changes in breathing (higher, faster, or not at all), faster movements, feelings of anxiety, frowning, voice tone changes (usually higher, faster, or louder), an emotional charge building up, or stomach tension. Look for these clues in your behavior: emotional eating, upset with others, focusing attention on and judging others' behavior, self-righteousness, being demanding or defensive, blaming others, or complaining.

Here is a list of more words and qualities that can be associated with being in control versus being in a place of surrender. The degree to which you experience these in your life will help you know whether you live your life trying to be in control or have opened to surrender.

- *Control:* rigidity, limiting, fixed, hard, confining, dominating, fitting in, expectations, attachment, manipulative, defensive, reactive, intolerant
- *Surrender:* flexibility, allowing, flowing, spontaneity, aliveness, radiance, forgiveness, empathy, compassion, creative, softness, openness, playfulness, out of the norm.

For years I didn't see myself as controlling, at least I didn't think I was trying to push people around or control their behavior. However as I achieved a greater understanding of how the controller operates, I started to recognize that I *did* act to control things. I exhibited controlling behavior with external circumstances by exhibiting tense and anxious responses to the twists and turns of life. When things didn't go as I expected, I became upset. When my daughter acted obnoxious, I behaved in kind. When sudden financial crises occurred, I became exceedingly tense. In my relationships with others, I was often defensive. Outwardly, many of these reactions were not apparent, I appeared cheerful and friendly. But inwardly I was experiencing anxiety. Often I expressed that anxiety by going a hundred miles an hour. In fact, I had my life set up with so much to do that I had very little time or energy left to stop and feel what was really going on. Do-aholism creates so many distractions that one no longer experiences one's true feelings.

When the controller is trying to keep circumstances or people under control, it is doing it's job of "external controlling." When it tries to protect us from experiencing our uncomfortable feelings, those of anger, sadness, hurt, fear, loneliness, helplessness, dissatisfaction, or not wanting to be here, it is doing it's job of "internal" controlling.

> *Experiencing feelings is basically a nonlinear, out-of-control activity. It is necessary to be out of control to really feel.*

The controller has countless ways to protect us from painful feelings. This might be advantageous except for the fact that with this intense first line of defense against experiencing "bad" feelings comes a blocking of our more desired feelings such as joy, spontaneity, and love. In doing this, the controller limits our connection with Spirit as well as access to our creativity and guidance. It does this by: 1) not letting us express our feelings that help us create our sense of aliveness, and 2) not allowing us to be spontaneous, which inhibits our free co-creative flow with the universe. By accepting what life brings us, good or bad, allowing ourselves to feel deeply and then move on, we open our lives to flow, a sense of ease, and inner peace.

The normal modus operandi of our culture, that is, everything in control, breeds struggle, stress, illness, and suffering. Learning to live with this new way of thinking, which embraces surrender, in the midst of our modern active lives, is, I believe, a key to turning our world around—not only our inner world and its resulting outer manifestations but also our planet.

Vulnerability

Learning to let go of control and surrender also involves opening to our vulnerability. In our culture, vulnerability has gotten a bad rap. It is to be avoided at all costs. But, in fact, learning to be vulnerable has many benefits. As we let go of defenses to our own emotions and discover that it is safe to do so, we can walk through life without so many walls and facades. We then appear more authentic because we *are*, and we are also much stronger in that we are more flexible. We are actually safer than when we construct rigid walls for protection, because when those walls are penetrated they can break. When we learn to come from a place of vulnerability, we have more resilience when things occur that we do not like. Thus we are much better off because it is impossible to completely prevent the storms of life from blowing. We become like the willow tree, which can bend and not break in a storm. If we are subject to feelings of hurt, loss, or frustration, they can flow through us more quickly and fluidly than when we resist or try to defend ourselves against such feelings. Allowing our vulnerability is more gentle on us in the long run.

Another benefit of allowing ourselves to be more vulnerable is that it helps us understand others' feelings and creates compassion. Sometimes this can lead to healing and harmony between people, where previously there was discord. It happened for me as a final stage to a long process of healing with my former husband. Allowing myself to be vulnerable to his feelings is what opened the space that let us finally be friends after eleven painful years of separation. I had been working on the issues that our relationship brought up and trying to take as much responsibility as I could for my part—mostly through an intellectual process of understanding. But one day I really let myself experience my feelings of sadness and remorse for the people I had shut out of my heart by constructing a wall of defenses. From that place of vulnerability I was able to feel and understand what my former husband had been feeling when we were together. Sure, he did plenty of things I could be angry about, but I suspended that and let myself feel things from his perspective— not just understand them but actually *feel* them. The day after this happened, for the first time since we were married he looked me directly in the eyes. I never said anything, but somehow I had opened a space in my heart that he was able to feel. A few weeks later, I shared with him what I had felt and my remorse for how I had been. As a result, the wall of hate that he had held for me finally lifted. Not long after this we actually joined forces in a business venture and lived under one roof for a while as friends, which seemed to me nothing short of a miracle. Though there were other steps in this healing process that I will describe later in the book, I believe it was my vulnerability that had the greatest single impact on this situation. Allowing yourself to be vulnerable can seem scary or strange, but it is worth the risk because it can open you to real magic in your life.

Universal Creative Power

One principle that is essential to the ability to surrender is belief in a universal power that works within, around, and through us. I often use the word *Spirit,* or *Divine Source,* but there are many names for this energy: God, Goddess, Great Mother, Universal life force, Christ, Buddha, Great One, Allah, Mother Earth. On the path of truth, there are no exclusions. You are free to believe whatever honors your truth and feels right to you. Some say that we are one with this power, while others claim it is greater than us. From whatever perspective you experience this great, wise, and loving energy, the key is to have trust and faith in it as a powerful, benevolent, and creative source. This source of energy wants for us only our greatest good—and ultimately, the greatest good for all. As we learn to surrender to the support that is available through this trust, we gain an ever-increasing ability to let go of the need to "hold up the fort" ourselves. Life is exhausting when we are trying to do everything on our own—to make things happen or stop things from happening.

My old tendency was impatience and the inability to trust that things really would work out if I didn't do everything my self. That lack of trust was a reflection of my lack of faith within myself and a disbelief that I would ever really be supported from without. I felt I had to carry the load myself and "make" life happen. Trying to push the boulder up the mountain alone was exhausting and led to a lot of futile effort. But by working with the tools I've written about in this book, I gained a deeper sense of trust. This expanded sense of trust and learning the fine art of surrender brought me to a place where I had faith in the flow of life and the support of a greater energy. From this new place, much of the struggle in my life has disappeared; instead, I spend more of my time in a state of peace and inner relaxation.

When we learn to surrender to the flow of life, things feel easy and even fun. Support may appear in our lives as things we are successfully able to manifest from our own efforts, help from others, creative inspiration, or serendipitous circumstances that seem to occur miraculously.

We let ourselves be supported by stepping out into the unknown, trusting, then finding that we are caught by an invisible safety net. As our positive references for being caught increase in number, our sense of trust grows. As our trust grows, we are able to let go more and experience a greater sense of ease. After a while the concept of struggle becomes a thing of the past. From this relaxed and open place, the opportunity for creativity and full expression is heightened.

Embarking on such an adventurous journey as exploring the unknown, learning to surrender, and letting go of control, might require a good carrot at the end of the stick. I can assure you with the confidence that comes from personal experience and from the experiences of many others, that nothing yields greater results in life—both inner results of peace and outer results of balanced success.

Learning the subtle yet powerful art of surrender and letting go of control holds a magic key to living the life of our authentic self. We begin to fully live each day and every moment in co-creation and concert with our divine connection to Spirit. Living our lives this way opens the door to creativity, passion, and aliveness.

TRY IT!

1 | Accessing Your Controller

Before we attempt to move in a new direction, we must be aware of what is limiting us. The following questions, if approached in a quiet, open and willing space, can reveal a lot. Do not use the answers to these questions to judge or blame yourself; rather, use them to become mindfully aware. Sometimes the awareness alone can cause things to shift. In addition, awareness serves as a strong motivating force for conscious behavior change.

❑ Find a quiet place and time to be absolutely honest with yourself in answering the following questions. Sometimes it is helpful to do this out loud with a friend. Answer spontaneously and let your friend jot the answers down for you. If you are doing these alone, it is best to write your answers.

❑ How do you react when things, others, or circumstances don't go the way you want them to?
Example: I experience internal anxiety and tension, I raise my voice, give up, feel sorry for myself, anger, impatience.

❑ How do you react when something unexpected happens that doesn't meet your preferences? (regarding money, time, order, etc.)
Example: I rage, complain to everyone, become tense, take it out on others.

❑ What actions do you most often take to avoid experiencing your deepest feelings?
Example: I stay very busy, exercise compulsively, drink, blame others, withdraw, remain angry.

Express Yourself
36

❑ What are typical situations or actions of others that trigger your controller?

Example: When my spouse leaves a mess, when people drive too slowly.

❑ How does "the controller" most commonly play out in your life?

Example: When I get behind on my list of to do's I get irritable and tense, wanting to solve others' problems, telling others how it "should" be done.

❑ How do you attempt to control others in your life, especially those close to you?

Example: By raising my voice and becoming intimidating, telling others how it should be done, becoming helpless, playing the victim, being the drama queen.

2 | Being Quiet and Learning to Not Do

❑ If you find yourself either talking a lot during the day or dominating conversations, consciously choose for a period of time (an hour, a day, a week) to say very little and just listen to others. If you like the experience and the results, do this more frequently and longer.

❑ Set aside a regular period of time each day to sit alone quietly. The time could be only five minutes, but regularity is very important. Be realistic and begin on a small scale so you can stick with it. You can sit and watch your breath go in and out, look out at a nature scene, or pick a formal meditation practice. The key is to let your internal dialogue cease for at least a few minutes.

3 | Following the Impulse

Learning to act from our impulses rather than our "have-tos" or "should-nots" is a great exercise for cultivating our ability to be in the unknown. For most people, the tendency is to plan what we are going to do in advance of actually doing it or to do mainly things we feel we have to do. Of course such conscious actions have value, but when a person acts out of these motivations to the exclusion of all other possibilities, experiences are diminished. It is important to also learn how to move through life in the state of being fully present in the moment.

❑ For a day, part of a day, or even an hour, sit with no plan. Ask yourself, "What do I feel like doing?" When you get an impulse to do something, act on it (for example, reading a book). When you have acted on that impulse and no longer feel like continuing to read, see where the next impulse takes you. Let yourself move from one impulse to the next. Be willing to do nothing for as long as it takes to feel the next directive that comes from inside. As you wait, periodically ask yourself, "What do I really want now?" It is possible to be moved to do some work; if that is the case, check where your impulse is coming from before you dive in. Ask yourself, "Am I acting out of obligation, or is this a true impulse of what I want to do?" You may be inspired to do activities that you normally do for fun, but don't be surprised if you unexpectedly get an impulse to do very quiet or simple things. Whatever the impulse, only follow it for as long as you desire, then stop and wait for the next impulse. If you like this experience, gradually schedule longer periods for such play—perhaps an entire weekend, a week, or even longer.

four
Reestablishing Trust with Self

One of the first steps to fully knowing and expressing our truth is to develop a relationship of trust with ourselves. When we trust ourselves fully, all parts of our being are willing to support our truth. Developing trust within ourselves is a step-by-step process. Just as it takes a lot of love for an abused child or a beaten dog to trust someone without flinching, so it is with our inner being. We have spent years telling our inner-selves what we should or shouldn't feel or do, often putting everyone else first, so it is understandable that reestablishing a relationship with ourselves can take some time and focus.

Establishing levels of trust within ourselves begins with opening up lines of communication. It involves a gentle coaxing process, and one of the keys to doing this is never to force or push. I worked with a woman who had spent years focusing on her personal growth, taking many workshops, reading self-improvement books, and seeking counsel. Though she had reached a place of great awareness and understanding, when it came to experiencing feelings, knowing her own truth, and living a creatively expressive life she had a long way to go. Part of the problem was that she was always "making" herself do things that she thought would help her grow, thereby telling herself she was not good enough as she was. Also, in her zealous efforts at improvement, she often missed opportunities to play and nurture herself. Consequently, the process was at odds with the goal; her forcefulness undermined the very thing she desired. Eventually she learned to let herself know that she was valued for who she was in each moment and began to heed the desires of her inner self instead of always doing what she had logically decided was best. After making these shifts and practicing other tools in this book, she was able to lead a creative and fulfilling life.

There is much talk these days about the *inner child*—that aspect of our inner being that has desires, feelings, and emotions. Directly related to the emotional body, the inner child often holds *frozen energy* relating to difficult past experiences such as traumatic incidents or unhappy conditions that occurred over a period of time. I call this aspect of the inner child, the *unhappy child*, and some call it the *adaptive child* because it has adapted many beliefs and modes of behavior to protect itself. Although such defensive devices may have helped the child adapt to unpleasant situations, they no longer serve the adult. By developing an awareness of these old behaviors, lovingly counterbalancing them, and spending time giving active love and attention, the unhappy child can be transformed into the *nurtured child*. The health and happiness of the inner child is extremely important because it determines the capacity for playfulness, spontaneity, creativity, and a general feeling of aliveness and joy. In addition, it is said that our inner child is our direct link to our intuition. Thus, as we open the channels to a happy and nurtured inner child, we simultaneously open the way to our higher creative self.

Not OK Messages

The process of regaining trust in ourselves and cultivating a nurtured child involves becoming aware of the programming that stands in the way of taking care of ourselves. Our tendency is to judge ourselves as not good enough. We further condemn ourselves for thoughts, behaviors, and feelings that society, or we personally, have decided are bad—sexuality, emotions like anger or sadness, or putting our needs ahead of others.

Most of us have internalized the message that it is not OK to desire something for yourself. We learned that to gain acceptance and approval we needed to fulfill the desires of others. If we give our desires a priority, we are labeled "selfish," particularly if our needs are contrary to the needs of others. In fact, there are a number of "not OKs" that were handed down to most of us, from our parents and society.

The following is a list of more "not OK" messages that has been adapted from John Gray's *What You Can Feel You Can Heal*.[4]

- Not OK to appreciate yourself

  If you are too open and honest about self-appreciation, it is considered vanity, and you are labeled "conceited." As a child you quickly learned what is common and acceptable is false humility or self-denigration (i.e., "Oh, I am so ugly").

- Not OK to be yourself

  This is the message that you must "earn" love, your beingness is not enough. Your value is connected with your abilities, appearances, productivity or anything you *do* rather than your inherent "beingness"—where you are already enough. This message was often learned in situations where there was approval for certain behaviors but an abrupt withdrawal of love or acceptance when behavior didn't measure up to expectations. Those who have received this message often focus on doing or become people pleasers.

- Not OK to make mistakes

  Any mistake you made was cause for abrupt withdrawal of love or approval or you were compulsively corrected. Those who received this message focus on their imperfections, have a lot invested in not wanting to be wrong, and can be very defensive. When approval is given they may not trust it or believe it.

- Not OK to express oneself

  Whenever any form of expression became too loud, boisterous, or departed from the acceptable norm, there was strong disapproval or punishment. Also expression of feelings such as anger, sadness, fear, or sexuality may have been shunned. Thus the individual learned to hold back or shut down. When we are constantly trying to please others or control ourselves to maintain safety, win approval, or avoid reprimand, the focus is on fitting the mold of what we "should be." Hence we lose our inherent ability to express creatively who we are or what we really feel.

All these negative messages lead to the same unfortunate out-come—a downward spiral of not knowing who you really are and, worse yet, not trusting yourself. The inner child doesn't trust that it's expression will be heeded or listened to with an open loving attitude. This is true especially if there is either conscious or unconscious self-judgment regarding the not OK messages or any other falling short of expected ways of being. As a result, rather than being our-selves we take on an idealized self that fits into the expected norm or some other standard. The way to help your inner child regain trust is to actively counteract these negative messages.

When we make ourselves wrong for not being the way we are "supposed to be," we may take on an exaggerated version of how we think we are supposed to be. We take on characteristics, or *personas* and become stuck in these behavior patterns (discussed more in Chapter 7 and 14). For example, you might operate as the *nice person* who puts on a sugary grin no matter what they are feeling, the *asexual* who hides their sensuality, the *quiet one* who can't speak up, the *overresponsible* who always has too much to do and not enough time to do it, or the *perfectionist* who is constantly nitpicking. The behavior can also become its unhealthy extreme. For example, desiring for ourselves becomes greed; an-ger is expressed as harmful attacks on others; or sexuality be-comes unloving or violent. To be on the path of truth means to accept ourselves fully, including behaviors or feelings we don't like. This does *not* mean condoning or approving bad behavior but approving of ourselves as people behind the behaviors, thoughts, or feelings. In conscious parenting they call it separating the child from the behavior. In other words, although you can *do* wrong, you can't *be* wrong.

Conscious Acceptance

Part of the process of regaining the trust of your inner being and regaining your wholeness, is practicing regular *conscious acceptance*—first becoming aware of your inner dialogue, actions, feelings, or desires, then dropping all negative internal judgment and counterbalancing it with kind or loving internal self-talk. For ex-ample, when you say something critical to yourself, whether inter-nally or out loud, consciously cancel this judgment, lovingly tell yourself that it is OK, and make an understanding remark. Every time you notice yourself acting, thinking, or feeling in some way you find objectionable, or would prefer not to be engaged in, stop and tell yourself, "I love you; I accept you in your fear, jealousy, insecurity, dishonesty, and so forth. I prefer that we change this behavior, *and* I love you." This exercise focuses on loving ourselves in our "untogetherness" with all our imperfections rather than conditionally loving ourselves only if we fit a perfect model.

In *Learning To Love Yourself*, Gay Hendricks offers many effective exercises for learning how to bring conscious acceptance to all that we are and do. I had a great opportunity to use one of these exercises to deal with my own behavior. One of the strong messages I received growing up was that it was a sin to waste money. When I was ready to buy a new car, I fell into one of my patterns, impulsiveness. Because I was eager to get what I wanted, I went to the first place, made a poor deal, and bought a car. The next day I discovered I could have purchased it for much less at another place, but since I had driven the car off the lot the dealer would not take it back. Due to my impatience I lost a large sum of money and could not stop criticizing myself. Finally, practicing one of the exercises in the book, every time I became critical for my mistake, I would say to myself, "I love you, even for being impulsive and impatient." During this same time period, others had occasionally become disgruntled with me for changing my mind about things. This was especially hard on me because I was a chronic people pleaser, and disappointing others gave me good cause for self-negation. So I would counteract this tendency by repeatedly saying to myself, "I love you, even when you change your mind." *

By practicing this conscious acceptance every opportunity I could, over time I felt a noticeable shift. The inner critical voice and feelings associated with it calmed down and with this I experienced more self confidence and the courage to take risks. In addition, as I practiced listening to myself with more awareness and speaking kindly to myself—lovingly accepting every aspect of my being—it

---

* This is a variation of Gay's exercise, which is to say, "I love you for changing your mind," changing the *even when* to *for*. Either variation communicates essentially the same positive message to the self which says, "I love you no matter what you do or don't do."

felt like removing a heavy weight that I had been dragging behind me and I began to experience forward movement.

Self-acceptance is an important step in regaining trust in ourselves and making positive changes in our lives. Practicing self-acceptance means heightening our awareness of what we think and say to ourselves, then consciously choosing to be understanding and compassionate. This requires replacing any judgmental or harsh language in our minds with kind words, even in circumstances that we believe are reproachable. By continuously speaking to ourselves in this loving manner and continually accepting what we are doing, feeling, or saying, our inner being becomes less afraid to express its truth and this builds courage.

In addition, when our inner being feels accepted and not judged, the lines of communication begin to open. We can then "hear" or know more clearly what it is feeling, what it's desires are, and what is good for us to do or not do. Then we can tell the difference between the essence and the form of things, that is, we are not fooled by the appearances of circumstances or people. We can then bring more of what is good into our lives and avoid what is not.

Forgiveness

Acceptance of every aspect of ourselves, along with acceptance of others, is the foundation for a creative and fulfilling life. Forgiveness is an act that can be incorporated into acceptance. Acceptance is the all-embracing attitude that allows for things to be the way they are, and forgiveness is the act of declaring your intention to accept and let go of any negative energy or blame you may be holding toward yourself or others.

> *Forgiveness is an act of love; it says, "I am willing to be bigger than my resentment, disappointment, judgment, or hurt." When you forgive, you lighten the field and make space for something new.*

To forgive before you have accepted the feelings you are holding, however, is like an idle promise, a nice idea that will not allow a shift to occur. It is glossing over the top of the issue while ignoring what is going on underneath. If not honored, those feelings underneath will surface to haunt you in one way or another, no matter how good your intentions are. Only by first feeling or acknowledging your anger, hurt, or sadness, can you come to a true place of compassion. Then your forgiveness will have more meaning and truth in it.

It is a good idea to approach forgiveness as a ritual. Your ritual could be as simple as writing a letter to yourself or someone else stating all your feelings, including your forgiveness; you can either give this letter to someone or not. You could state your forgiveness while standing alone in nature, at an altar or any other special spot. Perhaps telephone an estranged friend or relative, or go talk to them in person. To perform this ritual with someone who is not alive, or whom you do not feel ready to face, use a surrogate. In this case, it is best to sit face to face with the surrogate, looking in their eyes yet seeing the actual person you are forgiving in your mind's eye. The surrogate can either respond with periodic thank yous or express what the higher self of that person might say.

Begin your forgiveness ritual by stating how you have been feeling. Follow up by declaring your forgiveness. Remember this is about letting go of all blame. Remember to also forgive yourself for whatever part you may have played, or for holding feelings of separation. However you choose to enact this ritual, let your intention be to forgive and let go.

Forgiveness of others and forgiveness of self are intricately related. Every time we practice acceptance and forgiveness of another it is as if we have practiced accepting ourselves. The inner being feels safe that it will be accepted when it experiences you extending this to others. It also works the other way around. Having practiced self acceptance for some time now I have noticed people feel safe with me. On some level other than conscious they know I will accept them without judgment because I am doing the same for myself.

As you practice conscious acceptance and forgiveness regularly, your inner being begins to trust you, and you gain a new ally, a friend that will open up new aspects of yourself. This openness is a key to intuitive knowing as well as the ability to tap your creativity. The practice of love and acceptance is the foundation for all the others.

TRY IT!

1 | Not OKs

❑ Make a list of all the things that are "not OK" with you, including emotions, actions, ways of being, and parts of your body. Write as quickly as you can without thinking or censoring. Some items will be things you know you believe are not OK, while others will be things you may consciously think are OK but subconsciously believe are not.

2 | Practicing Conscious Acceptance

❑ Pick five key items from your "not OK" list and fill in the following sentences with each one. Do this in front of a mirror, look straight into your eyes and repeat out loud:

  ❑ "I love you for being (or doing) ___." (Know that you are not condoning what ever it is, just accepting yourself unconditionally.)

  ❑ If you choose, you can try other variations:
  "I love you even with ___."
  "I accept you in your ___ (the state or way of being you previously judged)."

  ❑ Eventually do this with all the things on your list that you feel strongly about.

❑ In your everyday life, notice what you do, say, or feel that is one of your "not OKs." When you notice this, say one of the preceding phrases to yourself.

3 | Forgiveness

This process will allow you to shift the form of any relationship—mother, father, friend, or partner. It does not necessarily mean that you are ending the relationship, unless you already have or want to. It is a commitment to change the existing dynamic by bringing acceptance and forgiveness into it. This can be done as a letter, which you can burn in a ritual of letting go or send, sitting at an alter or best, looking into the eyes of the person you are working with or a surrogate. You can do this with someone who is currently in your life, someone you never see, or has deceased. It is also powerful to do this with yourself.

❏ Breathe together, looking in each other's eyes, deeply and fully, together or alternating.

❏ Remember and express earlier times or special events when the love was freely flowing. Recall what was good and special about them (or still is).

❏ Begin compassionate communication from the heart, expressing the truth of your entire range of feelings. While maintaining eye contact, use the following questions as a guide.
  ❏ Communicating Feelings
      What I haven't communicated to you
          is ___.
      What I am most afraid to tell you
          is ___.
      The feelings I have held are ___.

  ❏ Taking Responsibility
      I apologize for any unloving communications or actions I have directed towards you, such as ___.
      I admit these are my issues I am working out and ___.
      I am now willing to let go of blame and making you wrong.

47

❑ Forgiveness

What I most need to forgive you for is ___ or, I
forgive you for not being ___ or doing ___.
What I most want you to forgive me for
is ___.
I forgive myself for ___.

❑ Love and Understanding

I love you because ___.
Thank you for being a teacher for me, for
helping me see the unseen in me and love
the unloveable in myself.
I understand that ___.
I love and honor myself for ___.
I am most grateful for ___.

❑ Intentions

My loving intention is ___.
What I most want is ___.
I pray the best for you, for your happiness
and ___.

End with any other loving statements you feel called
to make and a hug if possible. Let yourself sit with the
feelings that will probably come up in doing this process.

chapter five

Freeing Yourself by Feeling Your Feelings—

The Doorway to Your Truth

One way we lose the trust of our inner being is through constantly ignoring, denying, or talking ourselves out of what we really feel. This behavior begins when we are young: when we shut down in order to make a painful household bearable; at school where we may have felt forced to learn in a manner that was foreign to us; or, to maintain social acceptance. This behavior continues as we grow older: at the workplace, where we may compromise who we are just to survive or to support the material lifestyle to which we have grown accustomed; in our relationships, where we fear others' judgments or reactions to our expression of what we actually feel. Thus, we become conditioned to closing the door on our true feelings.

In our daily life we regularly tell ourselves not to feel what we are feeling. For example, if you feel angry at someone for what they are doing, rather than tell the person what doesn't work for you, you may say, "Oh, that's OK." Or you may tell yourself it is ridiculous to be upset about a particular thing, without acknowledging your true feelings about it. Or when something constantly hurts you or frustrates you, you may tell yourself to just live with it for fear of upsetting the apple cart. You ignore any feelings you have about a situation or if you do notice them, you tell yourself all the reasons why you shouldn't be feeling them. All this is called *discounting* your feelings—making them less than they are.

Susan came to me because of troubles she was having in her relationship. Her boyfriend Mark consistently criticized and spoke harshly to her. Occasionally he would see other women, and gave her little affection. Yet she was expected to keep the house, make the meals, and bring in half the income. Susan tolerated this for a long time because she was afraid that Mark would leave her. She became increasingly depressed from denying her own feelings of frustration, hurt, and anger. Eventually she could no longer ignore her feelings.

Susan presented a classic example of "fear of abandonment," although in actuality she had abandoned herself through years of denied and discounted feelings. In such circumstances it's no wonder we don't want to be left alone, for no one would be there for us, not even ourselves. We would truly be alone, and that can be scary.

Over time, Susan was able to nurture herself and express her feelings. As a result, she learned how to take a stand on her own behalf and take care of herself. Susan eventually left the relationship since she no longer feared being without a partner as she grew to trust and love herself.

This kind of strength and inner trust develops from creating a loving relationship within ourselves. Honoring and accepting our feelings is an essential part of the process. However, to stop discounting our feelings, we must first become aware of when and how we do it.

How many times have you looked back at a problematic circumstance and said to yourself, "I knew it, something told me not to do that," but you didn't pay attention to this feeling. How many times have you felt an emotion or reaction to someone's behavior but told yourself it wasn't right to feel that way or rationalized the feeling by saying, "they meant well, they couldn't help it or that person has been so good to me, how can I be angry?" or "I'm a spiritual person, I should be bigger than this." We have an endless repertoire of rationalizations we use to convince ourselves we should not feel the way we do.

What We Resist Persists

We often avoid feelings that we judge to be less desirable or socially unacceptable, such as anger, hurt, sadness, or fear. Unfortunately, this tactic does not work because what we resist persists—what we try to block from our experience is intensified.

For example, a man named Richard was often plagued by jealousy. He regularly fantasized that his girlfriend would leave him for another man. Each day he would wake with feelings of anxiety relating to these fears. Although he realized they were irrational, the more he despised such feelings, and tried to ignore them, the more intense they became. He used avoidance tactics such as keeping busy, eating, or demanding that his girlfriend ease his fears with constant physical closeness. He ended up pushing her away since she withdrew from this clutching, thereby creating the very situation he feared.

My mother used to say "just rise above it," in essence telling me to ignore any uncomfortable feelings. However, this philosophy did not work well for her as my mother died an early death from the affects of her addictions, which were her attempt to ignore it all.

There can also be other consequences of denying uncomfortable feelings. When we hold back feelings that we label undesirable, we also hold back the full expression of feelings we consider desirable. Our entire range of feelings is comparable to a big pot of soup—they're all in there together. We can't express true joy while we're holding down anger, even anger we're not fully aware of. Although we can pretend to be having a good time, we cannot express a pure state of happiness without first lifting the lid on the other feelings as well. We waste vital energy keeping a lid on uncomfortable feelings, which often results in depression and fatigue. Depression is repressed emotion, a blockage in the energy flow. Conversely, when we let ourselves feel our feelings, this allows the blocked energy to move and contributes to feelings of vitality and aliveness. This also helps build a relationship of trust between our everyday selves and our inner being.

> *One important key to opening the door to our inner being is allowing and accepting all feelings, including the uncomfortable ones.*

A number of tools and exercises to help you practice this are presented in Chapter 10.

Understanding More About the Emotional Body

The inner being communicates to us in two ways: through the subtle feelings and senses, including intuition, and through the physical senses of the body. Body messages can be gentle, or strong and painful, depending on our ability to listen. After years of paying very little attention, lines of communication diminish. As a result, the inner being either gives up and shuts down, which we experience as depression and fatigue, or it is forced to scream at us so we will pay attention, which it usually does through strong body messages. For example, when the inner being wants to tell us something such as, "I want a break; I want to play," if we refuse to listen and the desire is strong enough, the inner being may cause us to get sick or have an accident forcing us to stop working. Or if we feel fed up and sick to our stomachs of how someone is treating us, we may contract a stomach ache or intestinal pain. As we become adept at listening to and honoring our inner messages, the inner being can communicate in more gentle and subtle ways.

In addition, when emotions are not allowed expression at the time they are experienced, they become locked in the body—stored in the cellular memory of different organs and tissues. Not only is the energy of such emotion stored energetically, there is also a chemical reaction in the body. Just as endorphins are released with positive feelings, different hormones are released with other emotions. When these hormones accumulate, they are toxic.

This is clearly demonstrated with "Positron Emission Tomography," a test that creates a color picture of the brain showing various concentrations of different hormones associated with particular emotions. For example, when someone is angry, an area of the brain rich in the hormone norepinephrine will light up in a specific color. If someone is feeling hopeless, areas rich in the hormone dopamine will appear. It is interesting to note that these particular hormones suppress our immune function, affecting our ability to fight illness.

When we speak of emotions, we speak about energy. In other words, the emotional body is the more energetic component of us, while the body is the more physical aspect. When the emotional body is allowed to express freely without judgment, it is considered to be vibrating fully. The word *emotion* can be understood as "e-motion," energy in motion. When there is a lack of ability to be who we are or to express ourselves, the vibration slows down. This occurs for example, when we discount feelings, engage in self pity, judgment, blame, or generally resist any emotion. When this happens for a long period of time, we feel sluggish, depressed, and dispassionate.

When emotions are allowed to fully vibrate in a free-flowing manner, this is referred to as *wave energy*. Allowing wave energy to flow means letting ourselves experience an emotion without resistance so that it can move through us like a wave. When we practice allowing emotions to move through us rather than denying them, the emotion naturally dissipates in a shorter period of time than it might otherwise. We can even help it along with body-centered practices that involve moving, breathing, or sounding, as described in Chapter 10.

I like the distinction that Dr. William Glasser, author of *Control Theory*,[5] makes between what he refers to as "pure feelings" and "long-term feeling behaviors." Pure feelings occur in a relatively brief period when an experience triggers an immediate response or when emotional release work allows buried feelings to surface. When the feelings have been truly felt without resistance or judgment, they naturally dissipate. However, the usual reaction when emotions emerge is to contract within ourselves and resist them. There is also the tendency to start telling yourself stories about what you are feeling such as wallowing in self-pity—reactions which escalate or prolong the feelings. When you do this, you delay their natural flow and exhibit what Dr. Glasser calls long-term feeling behaviors, where you choose to continue to experience the feeling. Because the initial feeling just happened to you, you believe that the continuation of the feeling is also just happening to you, that you have no choice in the matter. Or perhaps you are receiving some benefit from being in the emotional state, such as getting attention, being taken care of, or not having to take responsibility. For these reasons, the emotion continues, leaving you unhappy and ineffective. Learning to "be with" our feelings, that is, to let them flow through us like a wave until they come to a natural completion, and then consciously and constructively releasing the energy, is a powerful practice we can incorporate into our daily lives.

Emotions are one of the nonlinear, less-structured aspects of the being associated with the *right brain* or feminine part—not feminine in terms of gender but in terms of yin and yang principles, which both genders possess. Yin energy is magnetic or "that which brings in." By contrast, yang energy is radiant or "that which goes out." An interesting aspect of a fully-vibrating emotional body is that, being yin energy, it has the ability to magnetize people, places, and things to you. In other words, as the emotional aspect of your being is allowed to be fully expressed, its vibrational frequency accelerates, as well as its ability to magnetically attract to you that which is right and true for you—for example, work that feels right to you or positive relationships that support you. When situations or people not right for you present themselves, if your vibrational frequency is accelerated, you have more sensitivity and awareness to distinguish them from those that are right. Thus, becoming more aware of your feelings and expressing them supports you in choosing circumstances that are right for you, while avoiding those that are not.

Another important aspect of emotions is how they relate to our belief systems. As long as you are resisting feelings, whether old or current and whether you know you are resisting them or not, you are trapped by the old beliefs and behaviors that are associated with these feelings. It is emotional experience that locks our beliefs in place. For example, our beliefs about life, people in general, men, women, or money are fixed by the emotions and feelings we experienced when we repeatedly saw something happen, when we heard phrases said over and over, or when a major traumatic event occurred. You make mental decisions as a result of these emotional experiences. You can work to transform the beliefs through mental exercises, but if the emotional core remains, you will be plagued by the effects of these beliefs. Consequently, you can work to change a life situation only to find yourself repeating the same pattern. Thus, working to change the beliefs alone, through affirmations, hypnosis, or other mind-oriented techniques, will often prove to be only partially effective. Although such techniques may change beliefs that have not been locked in by emotions, altering the beliefs that developed when emotions were involved usually requires getting to the root or core emotion associated with them. Examples of such beliefs are "I'm not good enough," "I am not worthy," "I am not lovable," "I do not deserve to be here," and "I am defective." (See Chapter 10 for further discussion of beliefs.)

Unfortunately, it is common to be totally unconscious of deep emotions from the past and their associated limiting beliefs because our mental defense systems are so good at hiding them. For example, you may think your relationship with a parent is fine, while simultaneously a part of you is angry or resentful. Although you may be able to say, "They just are who they are, they don't upset me anymore," the emotional scars of the past still remain.

For example, I worked with a man who had a persona of *nice guy* and followed a pattern of having, what he called, controlling women in his life. He was highly sensitive to any type of controlling behavior and would greatly upset him, or as he said, "it really pushes my buttons." In discussing his mother, he talked about how wonderful she was and how generous of her time and energy she had been all his life. But when asked to elaborate it became apparent that she was also overbearing and controlling in her care of him. While growing up he had difficulty learning from his own mistakes because she was always correcting him and making sure that he did things "right." Not only did he harbor anger and resentment about this, which he was unaware of, but it created a core belief that he was not capable—thus his attraction to capable yet apparently controlling women. Slowly he began to access the deep anger he felt regarding his mother's overbearing behavior. This was a difficult process because he felt guilty when he felt anything other than loving and grateful toward the woman who had "sacrificed" so much for him. Although he was strongly convinced that he could not possibly be harboring feelings of anger toward his mother, as he surrendered more to his emotional body's feelings, rather than his logical mind, he tapped a volcano of emotion. The degree to which he had resisted his feelings was paralleled by the intensity with which he released his anger. He spent much of the next day releasing anger from his intestines as well, something that can occasionally happen since the belly is the seat of our withheld feelings. After this releasing it was evident he had tapped into an empowered part of himself. He carried this forth into his life and later was able to firmly but gently speak his truth to his controlling girlfriend, set boundaries for himself, and function in a much more passionate and powerful way.

Most of us raised in this culture have some repressed emotional experiences even when our younger lives seemed relatively normal. You can access the truth of this by noticing the nature of your current daily life. If you are not passionately engaged in your work, fulfilled and satisfied in your relationships, or experiencing a general sense of peace, contentment, and joy, chances are you have some stored material to work with.

By allowing yourself to feel, know, and accept all aspects of your being, these emotions and the beliefs associated with them will begin to surface. The best way to access and release such beliefs and emotions is not by forcing them, but rather by complete surrender to and acceptance of what you feel day to day. As a result, the inner being will gradually feel safe enough to let you know what suppressed beliefs and emotions exist. (See Chapter 10 for further discussion and exercises on how to access and release these buried emotions.)

six
Learning to Actively Love Yourself

Here I am sitting at Makena-Little Beach, in Maui. The sun is shining, the water is sparkling, there are swarms of fish in their tropical splendor, and I am lying on the sand in my birthday suit feeling totally connected to nature, spirit, and life. Needless to say, I feel very content, but earlier this week things were very different. I had been occupied day in and day out with work-related projects and parental responsibilities. Although I try to spend at least a few hours in nature every few days, or a whole day at least once a week, it had been months since I had taken an entire day off. Somehow the world of doing and responsibilities had gotten its hooks in me again. Even on this lovely day I did some housecleaning and laundry. Does this sound familiar?

There is a sweet little girl in me who loves to romp and play, to be free and creative, and I have learned the hard way the price of not honoring her needs. When I don't make her a priority in my life, up there on the list with all the *have-tos* and *shoulds*, she eventually makes me aware of her displeasure by acting out in a number of ways: through grumpiness, headaches, or back aches; by illness or injury; or just by shutting down with depression or lethargy. Consequently, I have made her a very high priority in my life, although I admit that sometimes I slip back into the old ways, which diminishes the quality of my life.

Because I have had so much experience with a disgruntled, less than vibrant inner child, I have come up with a practical program for actively loving my inner child and maintaining her health, aliveness, and creativity.

When we work with this subject in my workshops, I ask people to ask themselves this question: if you were caring for a child and wanted to express love to that child, what would you do? Think of a child other than your own, because there's too much unconscious conditioning connected with parenting. Perhaps think of yourself as a loving grandmother. The responses to this question can then be applied to yourself.

This exercise purposely focuses on an external child because it is easier to think of caring for someone, apart from ourselves, than it is to think of caring for ourselves. We are taught that the only kind of giving that is OK is for others. In Chapter 4 we listed numerous not OK messages regarding giving ourselves attention. These are strong messages that make it clear why we have such a hard time making ourselves a priority and actively loving ourselves. If we do try giving to ourselves without having become aware of how such messages control us, we feel guilty and quickly abandon any program for self-care. Despite our best intentions, this guilt may sabotage any attempt to love ourselves.

With more awareness of these messages and the guilt that can intensify them, you can intentionally practice a few of the many possibilities for actively loving yourself. Becoming aware of the tendency to sabotage yourself will help you remain on course without self-judgment. Acting on any of these possibilities regularly will help you establish a more loving and trusting relationship between yourself and that part of yourself we call the inner child.

Possibilities for Actively Loving Yourself

Being Present

One of the usual responses to the question, "How would you make a child feel loved?" is, "I'd give that child undivided attention." We are usually so caught up in the "busyness" of our lives that we rarely focus on the needs of our inner child. So often we put all the shoulds, have-tos and responsibilities in our life first. When we do manage to spend time with the child (whether our inner child or an external one), often our minds are off in some distant place, thinking about a past event or worrying about the future. Consequently, even though we are physically there, the child does not feel our presence. One significant way to love your inner child is to be present, even if it is only for a few minutes each day. Just as focusing attention on a child even for a short time can have a powerful and lasting effect, so can a similar focus nourish your inner child. Whether meditating, gazing at a beautiful nature scene, or just noticing the feelings in your emotional or physical body, spending a short period of time being fully present each day can do wonders.

Spending Fun Time

Another point people mention regarding loving a child is making time to do something the child finds enjoyable—a practice that also nurtures your inner child. This means setting aside time to do whatever would please your inner child, letting it know that it is a priority and that you are serious about establishing a new relationship. As you practice this you will begin to experience definite changes in your inner child's behavior and attitude. I know that for me taking time to do enjoyable things has had a particularly strong, direct effect on my life.

It is important when scheduling an activity for your inner child, that it doesn't have a particular goal, just that it be something fun and enjoyable. Do what you love to do for its own sake, not for the benefit you are going to derive from it later. You do not have to be good at this activity. Often as children we enjoyed certain activities but weren't as good at them as some prescribed ideal, so we stopped doing them. The important thing is that the activity feels good to you and that you can lose yourself in it. Ask yourself what activity might you begin or get back to. Does a smile come to your face when you think about being in nature, playing sports, or doing something adventurous like skydiving or rock climbing? Or does doing something quieter like reading or playing chess bring you joy? Does dancing, singing, or painting sound like fun? Even if you have never done it before, it is never too late to start.

It is important to allow your inner child many avenues of expression. A child's favorite means of expression is often creative play through such things as music, song, dance, art, acting, sound, games, or poetry. These are also powerful modes of expression for our inner child. Spending a few hours doing any of these activities will enliven your inner child which will enliven you.

Getting back to basics by spending time in nature is another valuable activity—one that may or may not be considered fun time for you. Even if it is not, spending time in nature has a proven beneficial effect on the body and psyche. Although the wilder this natural environment is the better, even going to an urban park will be beneficial. Nature has a nurturing effect that cannot be compared to anything else. In our retreats, we take people out into the jungle and walk along streams and waterfalls which is an extremely foreign environment to people coming from urban environments and somewhat scary for a few. Nevertheless, such exercises have had a profound effect on all of them in a way that could not be matched by any other activity. Setting aside time to retreat to nature, whether once a week, a few times a month, or for an extended period each year, is an invaluable practice for nurturing your inner child.

Spending time with your inner child in any one of these playful, creative, or nurturing ways may require rearranging your priorities. If having a more loving relationship with your inner child and all the joy, aliveness, and creativity that it can potentially bring is a high priority for you then you will be willing to pay the price of eliminating or rearranging activities necessary to achieve this. There is an exercise at the end of the chapter to help you reassess your priorities.

Listen and Honor What You Hear

When the adults in my workshops discuss how they show love to a child, someone always suggests listening. Most people tend not to take the time to listen to their children—or their inner child—or don't listen attentively when they do. Although we may hear the words, we often don't focus on what the child is really saying or honor their feelings.

As I mentioned previously, honoring the feelings of our inner selves plays a big role in gaining trust in ourselves. We tend to discredit our inner selves and talk ourselves out of our own truth. This is lethal to our inner child since it discourages love and trust. Learning to listen and honor our feelings as well as those of other people can have a very positive effect on relationships. This is what happened for Justine and her daughter Carrie. Justine came to me because she was having difficulty with her daughter, Carrie. Although Carrie was only four years old, she carried a lot of inner tension and seemed to have great resistance toward her mother. Justine's problem with her daughter changed, however, when Justine began to fully accept her own feelings. Just as Justine's inner child began to trust her when she stopped trying to talk herself out of her own feelings, so did Carrie began to trust her mother as Justine started accepting her daughter's feelings. When Carrie encountered frustrating circumstances, rather than explain another way to look at it, Justine learned to reflect back the essence of what she had heard and empathize with her daughter's emotions. For example, instead of saying, "Well, I am sure Johnny didn't mean it," she would say "that must be really frustrating for you" or "you must feel angry." In this manner, Justine expressed to Carrie the feelings that had been conveyed, letting Carrie know she had been heard.

> *To truly accept and be comfortable with others' feelings, we must first practice being with and accepting our own.*

This is what had happened for Justine, resulting in a lasting positive effect on her relationship with her daughter.

It is amazing what this little tool, *compassionate listening*, versus playing Dr. Fix-it, can do for relationships in general. Compassionate listening involves not just listening to someone's words, but imagining what they might be feeling in that circumstance. Whether done in a business setting or at home in a more personal environment, this way of listening and responding not only enhances connection between individuals, but can defuse difficult situations. This is a very healing practice, not only for relationships with others but also for relating to ourselves. To actively love ourselves is to listen to our inner being and to honor, to the best of our ability, what is being communicated. We must see its needs, desires and thoughts as valid and respond accordingly. Although this may require some negotiating or rearranging in our lives, if the happiness of our inner being is a priority, we will be amply rewarded in feelings of creativity and happiness.

Many times in my own life I have not heeded messages from my inner child. My inner child has said, "Stop, I wanna go do something more fun!" But for my own compulsive reasons I did not stop or rearrange what I was doing. Then I noticed how irritable and tired I would become and remembered, "Ah, my child doesn't want to work this hard. This is my adult program. How can I make time for the needs of my inner child, too?" If I honor the needs of my inner child for an afternoon or even an hour, my spirits are so lifted that the activities considered drudgery before, become enjoyable. In addition, my inner child has feelings that are important to me regarding things other than play. I've even received communication from her about an unwise decision concerning an investment. The message came to me in the form of feelings about the woman I was to do business with. Unfortunately, I did not listen to these feelings because the business deal looked good from a logical and numerical perspective. Consequently I later ended up in a long and costly legal battle.

Some people may debate whether such messages are from the inner child or the intuition. I have heard it said that the inner child is the doorway to your intuition. I believe it does not matter if you call such a voice intuition or your inner child. The point is, it is important to honor and give credence to what the voice is telling you.

I am not suggesting we let our inner child dictate our lives, but rather that we bring some balance to our activities by giving our inner child greater attention. Sometimes it is necessary to negotiate between the strong feelings of your inner child and the desires of your adult self. For example, let's say you have an opportunity to do something fun for a weekend. But you also have an important business-related seminar you are scheduled to take on the same weekend. On the one hand, if you decide in favor of the enjoyable activities the child wins, but the adult loses. In this case you probably won't have that much fun anyway because you will be feeling guilty or worried. On the other hand, if you go to the seminar, the adult wins, the child loses. In this case, you may not get much out of the seminar, because you may get sick due to the inner child's resistance or be so distracted that you cannot concentrate. Thus, as long as you are in a win-lose situation, you never really win no matter what choice you make. Negotiation and compromise will help you find a balance. You might make an agreement to give your inner child something else it would enjoy, like taking time off during the week to go for a walk in the woods, or take two evening classes in something you love to do but keep putting off, in exchange for the child being fully present with you as you take your weekend seminar. When this happens, you will approach the seminar with a level of attentiveness that would not be possible without the enthusiasm of your inner child. Look for ways you can create a win-win situation between the two parts of yourself.

Communicate

It is also important to be aware of how we speak. Without realizing it, we often communicate to ourselves in derogatory phrases we learned from our family or society, using put-downs and tones of voice that inhibit the inner child. Unless we pay close attention and focus on catching and changing it, we will speak to our outer children as well as ourselves in these critical ways. (See Chapter 8 for further discussion of the "inner critic.")

A powerful exercise for communicating with your inner child is to regularly write her or him. Start off with something like, "What is going on for you?" or "What are you feeling about ___?" or just "What are you feeling?" Then let the words flow. You can respond, engaging in a dialogue, or just let the child speak freely. You will often be amazed at what comes out. If you have trouble getting in touch with your feelings, writing this way can be very helpful in building trust with your inner child. It lets him/her know that you care and that you are truly interested. Such an invitation to communicate, offered on a regular basis, opens the door for the child to express feelings closer to the time they occur rather than sitting on them for weeks, months or even years. This exercise also helps open the door to creativity. Julia Cameron, author of *The Artist's Way*,[6] believes regular journaling is an important tool for creative expression and recommends writing three pages about anything that comes to you every day without fail—calling these "morning pages."

Being Seen

Have you ever noticed how a child will often say "Watch me mommy" or "Look at me daddy." Children love to be seen expressing themselves, whether it is the excitement of flying down the slide, or the artistry of their dance to the beat, they want to be seen expressing what is fun or special to them. Our inner child feels the same way. But over the years with all the conditioning about how we are "supposed" to do things, we tend to shy away from having people watch us in our pure expression—unless we happen to be very outgoing or believe we are pretty "good" at something. If we can let go of having to meet certain standards, we can give our inner child a lot of love by letting it be seen in this way.

In workshops I have led, the participants have avenues for creative play such as making up something to sing, dance, or drum. They have opportunities to do any one of these activities one at a time if they choose. Even though it may only be for a few seconds and they may have some fear and trepidation at first, everyone who has let themselves be seen in this way is enlivened and full of joy after their expression has been witnessed.

Giving yourself opportunities to have someone watch you doing something you love is a powerful self love practice. My partner and I will sometimes just stand and watch while the other dances. Find ways you can have someone witness you in your expression. You could show a friend a project you are working on or ask them to sit while you sing a song—regardless of whether you think it is perfect or not.

In addition to having someone witness you in your joyful expression, it is also powerful to be seen in your feelings. For example if you are feeling a lot of sadness, just having someone witness your tears can be a very loving and healing act. Being seen can also be as simple as looking in someone's eyes and letting them "see" you. You don't have to "do" anything, such as projecting love, just let yourself be seen in your innocence and simplicity. Just as looking in the eyes of an infant lets the infant know it is loved, your inner child feels loved and accepted for who she or he is when someone maintains simple eye contact with you. You can even do this for yourself by looking directly into your own eyes in the mirror and thinking only loving accepting thoughts.

Being seen is about having the *essence* of you be seen and accepted—that which is simple and true about you rather than what you have constructed to help you cope or to look good in the eyes of the world. I have seen many people open up to very deep healing by looking into each others eyes. They allowed themselves to see and be seen in their essence with all their imperfections and humanness. Letting their barriers down and having their essence be accepted, touched a place in their hearts that had long been closed. Allowing ourselves to be seen in any of these ways not only heals old wounds but also allows us to feel safe to express more of our authentic selves in the world.

Living by Your Values

Webster says this about value: A principle, standard, or quality considered worthwhile or desirable; To prize, esteem; Worth in importance to the possessor; To rate according to relative estimate of worth or desirability. In general, values are what we deem important on our deepest level. They can be principles of living or they can be things we want to experience or have in our lives.

One of the things that makes a child feel safe and happy is congruence—that is honesty and consistency. When a parent says one thing and does another, this can be devastating to the child's self esteem. It doesn't know what to count on and it gets mixed messages about how to behave. For example, a parent may profess honesty but be sugary sweet and complimentary to the neighbor that she has complained about to the family and is even holding a grudge toward. The child is taught honesty by words but the parent is living out another value. What then does honesty really mean for that child? The child's ground becomes shaky and it doesn't know what it can trust. They might say they want to do something fun with the child but never make the time. The incongruences most of us have seen as children are numerous and taught us that it is normal to live by other than what we say is important.

It is the same with your inner child. Living in alignment with what you value—living in integrity, creates an environment of trust and safety that invites your inner child to come forth and raises your self esteem. To find what you really value you must put your cultural, parental and even religious conditioning aside. Sometimes your values coincide with what you learned and sometimes not. The more you practice all the tools in this book the more sensitive you become to knowing what is true for you. Ask yourself, "What do I love, what has meaning for me, what feels right and true to me?" The farther you live your life from your values, the harder, heavier or more out of sync life feels. The more congruent your life is with your values, the more in integrity and passionately alive you feel. Determine what is truly important to you, evaluate if you are living by those standards and then begin to make the changes necessary to start living in alignment with those values. To do this is an important, sometimes challenging, yet very powerful act of loving your-

self. (See Try It section for list of possible values and exercise to help with this.)

All of these practices increase in-the-moment communication from the inner child so that less withholding occurs. When there is less withholding and more open lines of communication, the inner child becomes stronger, healthier, and better able to support you in taking risks, such as communicating to someone what you are truly feeling. Your child becomes braver in supporting such risks because it knows it is safe with you—you will be developing inner courage.

As your inner child becomes emotionally stronger from your acts of love, she or he will support you in taking risks not only with others but also in the outer world. This enhances your ability do new things that reflect more of who you are. Such new activities may seem scary at first, but little by little as you start to have more "wins," and as you gain more trust and experience that you will be there to support yourself no matter what, you begin to move closer to a life that expresses your uniqueness. (See Chapter 16 for further discussion of this.) Multiplying acts of self-love increase your self-esteem and inner strength, which in turn support every aspect of your life.

TRY IT!

1 |Actively Loving Yourself Practices

The following exercises are meant to be integrated into your life on a regular basis—daily, weekly, or at least monthly. Pick any one or two to focus on for a while before adding others. When you practice any of these regularly, you will notice a distinct change in the way you feel, your energy level, your courage to take risks, and your ability to express yourself.

❏ **Be Present**

Give yourself a few minutes of focused quiet time each day. You might meditate, rest, stare out the window, or spend a few moments paying attention to what you are feeling in your body or emotions.

❏ **Fun Time**

Set aside regular time to do activities that you and your inner child feel are fun. It is important that you can lose track of time when you are doing this activity. You do not have to have recognized talent in this activity nor does it have to serve a purpose except enjoyment. (This practice and the next can be the same or different.)

❏ **Creative Expression**

Find an avenue of creative play, such as singing, dancing, music, art, poetry, or writing. Commit yourself to doing this a specified number of hours each week on your own or take a class. Classes are great not only to learn the skills involved but for the joy of doing what you love with others.

❏ **Nature Time**

Spend time in nature. Scheduling a specific time each week or month to do this enhances the likelihood that you will break out of your routine.

❑ **Listen**

Listen to what is going on in the recesses of your mind and emotional body. Ask yourself: "What am I feeling right now." When you get a response or any other communication from your inner being, be careful not to discount your feelings. Instead, practice "compassionate listening" as discussed in this chapter.

❑ **Honor Feelings**

Heed any internal messages to the best of your ability rather than dismissing them as unimportant, impossible, or otherwise invaluable. This may involve some negotiating, risktaking, or rearranging priorities.

❑ **Speak Kindly**

Listen carefully to your internal dialogue. When you hear harsh or judgmental words, derogatory tones, or other unloving expressions, counterbalance these with kind and loving words.

❑ **Writing**

Take time regularly to write your thoughts. This can either be done as 1) pure stream of consciousness, with no thought or concern about content, or 2) a dialogue between different parts of yourself, (e.g., you and your inner child). You can also bring other aspects into the conversation. Simply identify the aspect, such as aware self, loving parent, harsh parent, protector, critic, scared or otherwise adapted child, or nurtured child, and start writing to find out how various aspects experience a situation from their point of view. This is called *voice dialog* and should be done spontaneously without editing. Gaining clarity and honoring the feelings of the many different aspects of yourself is very nurturing and balancing.

2 | Exercises to Enhance Self Love

❑ **Intuitive Dialogue**

Set up a pillow, chair, or seat in front of where you are al-

ready sitting, letting this be the seat for your inner child. Move back and forth between these seats and have a discussion between you and the child. When you are in the child's seat assume a posture that best imitates the child's. The more you allow yourself to role play the child the better. It is best to do this out loud in a soft voice or whisper. Perhaps put on some gentle music that will support the process. You may want to put a stuffed animal in the child's seat to address your questions to. Imagine that your inner child is sitting there as you speak. The following is a list of questions to begin asking your inner child, then let your intuition guide you regarding what to ask or say. After you ask a question, move into the child's seat and speak for her or him. Write down key insights or commitments after you finish.
Possible questions:

❑ Are you willing to tell me what you are feeling?

❑ How can I help you feel safe enough to talk to me?

❑ How have you felt unloved by me?

❑ Have you felt I have discounted or ignored your feelings? If so, what are those feelings?

❑ What can I do to make you feel more loved or to honor your feelings?

❑ What can I do on a regular basis that you would enjoy?

❑ What changes would you like to see?

When you hear the child's responses to your questions, listen compassionately. Do not negate or discount suggestions or feelings. Conclude with some loving remarks or hugging the stuffed animal. When you are finished, make a list of the child's requests and do your best to make some changes that feel appropriate to you. Have these dialogues periodically. They can be very effective after emotional release (see exercises in Chapter 9) or during challenging times.

❑ Ideal Nurturing Parent

Find a comfortable, quiet spot, close your eyes, and relax. Allow an image to come forth of an ideal loving mother or father. Notice their hair, what they are wearing, their tone of voice, and so forth. Imagine yourself being held by them. Feel them rocking you. Now have them speak to you, hearing them telling you things you may have always wanted to hear from a parent. Perhaps confide in them about something that makes you feel bad about yourself. Hear their accepting and loving responses.

You can enhance this exercise in a number of ways. Having a friend you trust actually hold you is a powerful addition. If you do this exercise alone, you can hold a stuffed animal or pillow and imagine it is you being held by your loving parent.

Using this exercise, especially during times of distress, can leave you feeling soothed and nurtured, as if a real parent had actually supported you. Although doing this exercise only once is beneficial, doing it repeatedly makes an imprint on your emotional body that permanently raises your level of self-love.

❑ Being Seen

❑ Pick something you find enjoyment in such as dancing, singing, painting, skating, yoga, etc. Ask a friend to watch you from the most non-judgmental and accepting place in them selves. It doesn't matter how adept you are at the activity. What is important is to let go of any self criticism you may be holding and to do it with your enthusiasm and enjoyment.

❑ Sit facing someone you trust. Look directly into their eyes. Rather than staring, let the focus of your eyes be soft. Notice your tendency to smile or laugh at first. As you settle in and get beyond initial feelings of discomfort you will find it to be amazingly soothing. It is not uncommon for tears to arise from this level of vulnerability. Just let them flow as they are part of the healing.

This exercise is even more powerful if you have a group to work with. Simply spend a few minutes with one person then switch to someone else. It is best to have one person who calls the switch so you can all change at the same time. Soft music playing, or someone playing gentle guitar helps to create a nurturing environment.

If you do not have a group or another person that you feel comfortable doing this with, you can start by making a regular practice of looking in your own eyes in the mirror. As you do this notice the tendency to think judgmental thoughts. Gently switch them to accepting loving thoughts or simply say, "I love you." This may seem difficult at first, but stick with it and you will notice some positive results.

❏ Acknowledgment List
Make a list of everything you can possibly think of that you can acknowledge yourself for—traits, qualities, talents, physical features, capabilities, etc. Read this list to yourself often. If you are with a group have each person in the group take turns acknowledging you, either stand in the middle and receive this, or be lying down with eyes closed having them gently stroke your arms, legs, belly, forehead, face and hair as they speak to you. They will either speak out loud or whisper in your ear. Each person can take turns receiving in this way.

❏ Things To Consider—Writing Process
❑ What percentage of your activities, time, money, or resources is:
  • To fulfill obligations (shoulds, have tos, musts)
  • To solve problems (including problems with health,

money, work, children, or relationship)
- To become more ___ (some form of ambition)
- By choice
- For fun and enjoyment

❏ Write ten activities you love to do and list the amount of time (by week or month) you do these things.

❏ Values realignment

❏ List ten qualities or aspects of life that are most important to you or have the most meaning for you. Each one is considered a value. If you have a few that are similar you can make a "string" of related values and put them on one line.

❏ Next list these values in order of priority as they show up in your life now—reflecting how you actually live rather than how you would like to live.

❏ For each value ask yourself, "What price do I pay for having this value in this position?"

❏ Next reconsider what you really want in each position or write down any other values that might come up.

❏ Make another list that more closely represents the values you would like your life to reflect and a more accurate order of priority according to your truer desires.

Example
List 1—Values list
10 things most important to you. You can use the example below or the Sample List at the bottom of the page for ideas. Can be principles or things you want to do, be or have.

List 2—Values currently living
Prioritize as they appear in your life now
1. Career advancement, finances

"What price do I pay for having this value in the number 1 position?"

You might say, "The price I pay for having career and finances in the number 1 position is that my health is not very good, my relationship with my wife and kids is deteriorating and I am not experiencing peace of mind." Decide what is really important to you.

2. Health, diet, exercise/physical fitness

Ask, "What price do I pay for having this value in this position?" Work down the list this way.

3. Family, children
4. Relationship (husband, wife, partner)
5. Community involvement, social activities
6. Service
7. Sports
8. Spirituality, personal growth, inner peace
9. Nature time
10. Travel

List 3—Values redesigned

❑ After reflecting on this, make a new list based on your deeper truth or how you really want to be living your life.

❑ After making this second list, consider these questions:
- "What will I have to rearrange or give up in order to make the new values or positions of existing values a reality?"
- How will these changes improve my life in the long run?

Values: Sample List

This is a small list to give you ideas—the possibilities are endless:

- Spirituality • Partnership • Accomplishment
- Adventure/excitement • Leadership • Growth • Humor
- Risk taking • Trust • Loyalty • Convenience
- Environmentalism • Music • Playfulness • Sensuality
- To be known/intimacy • Honesty • Harmony
- Freedom • Security • Orderliness • Integrity
- Excellence • Privacy/solitude • Self-Expression

Discover Your
Deeper Self

PART
TWO

chapter **seven**

Recognizing and Regaining the Power in Your Shadow Self

As your inner being learns that it can trust you to accept its feelings and emotions without judgment, and as you take active steps to show your love, it will reveal more of its secrets. It will let be seen that which has been kept hidden in the recesses of your being and body. These secret, shut-away feelings and aspects of your being, as well as the less desirable behavioral characteristics associated with them, are referred to as the *shadow*.

What characterizes the shadow is that we judge it as unacceptable and relegate it to the dungeon of our consciousness. Thus a war goes on internally between the part that is regarded as unacceptable, wrong, or not enough and the part judging it as such. This internal split causes an on-going state of duality or separation within ourselves that prevents us from experiencing peace and self-love. To make matters worse, we project this split onto other things, circumstances, and people. Consequently, we blame others for their shortcomings and mistakes, or we blame things and circumstances for causing our problems—*projecting our shadow*.

The shadow must come into the light before you can experience wholeness. To *disown*—to deny any aspect of your being—ultimately holds you back from the full expression of yourself. Refusal to acknowledge the shadow self can wreak havoc in your life since these disowned aspects and feelings can surface in menacing and sometimes destructive ways. No matter how hard we try to cover them up or forget they exist, behaviors and reactions that are incongruous to who we think we are will ultimately crop up.

For example, Elizabeth, a strong, self confident, and capable career woman, had a recurring problem with relationships. She was bright and outgoing and had no trouble attracting men, but once she entered into an ongoing relationship, her shadow self would begin to surface. She would drive the man away with her clutching and neediness. Elizabeth's strong exterior was covering her scared, lonely, insecure child inside. Once she began to acknowledge this part of herself, experience the feelings associated with it, and allow it to exist without ridicule or disgust, she was no longer plagued by the way this aspect of herself would surface. Though this shadow self still existed, she was more open and honest about its presence. As it became acceptable to her, it no longer manifested in a way that was upsetting to her partners. Elizabeth's situation is common in romantic relationships.

> *Love acts as a bright light that illuminates and exposes our shadows. It flushes out everything unlike itself and the hidden truths begin to emerge.*

Even when not related to love and relationships, the shadow will cause people to act in ways incongruous with who they think they are, and to come across different than what they are attempting to project. For example, have you ever noticed someone putting on the air of "macho guy," though you can sense their deep-rooted insecurity. I call this the shadow coming out through the cracks.

Personas

The shadow refers not only to deeper feelings that we try to shut out or deny; it can also be any role we play that seems to serve us but actually traps us. These roles, called *personas*, reflect behavior characteristics that are a response to deeper feelings. Such roles are considered an aspect of the shadow because we are usually unaware that we are stuck in them. In Latin the word persona means the mask of the actor, and in this context, the character one sustains in the world. There is nothing wrong with such personas, which can be useful as part of a repertoire of how we choose to operate in the world. However, problems arise when we get stuck in them, unable to access the many other options available to us or to express our authentic selves.

These personas usually arise as adaptive mechanisms in childhood—as a means of winning love or approval or as a response to an unsafe or hostile environment. Thus, we become the roles we believe we are supposed to play, or have decided it is safer or more effective to play, instead of being our authentic selves. In this manner, we become narrower than we might otherwise be, limiting our range of self-expression. When we are unaware of how such roles control us, they form an aspect of our shadow.

The following is a list of examples of some of these roles or personas: nice guy or girl, super competent, helper, the victim, drama queen, the rebel, got it all together, Mr. Cool, seductress, independent, the teacher, enlightened one, the professional. Though some of these personas may just seem like jobs in life, it is not about what you do for a living, it is about how you carry yourself through life. It becomes unhealthy when we over identify with the role, forgetting the essence of who we are. Personas in and of themselves are fine when we can take them on and off like coats, using them as needed for specific purposes. However, if we are not aware that we are wearing the coat, then we are unable to take the coat off.

But why take it off if it is serving a useful purpose, you might ask. The answer is that being stuck in a persona has repercussions in our lives. For instance, being a helper seems innocent enough, but in order for the persona of the helper to exist, it needs a victim. By being wrapped up in the victim's problems, much of the helper's vital life force and creativity are wasted trying to help, and it provides a distraction from the helper's own self-awareness. In the long run the victims are not helped either, because they are supported in avoiding responsibility for their own problems. Each persona that derives from habit rather than choice has its own set of complex negative results. Thus, a powerful part of shadow work is to fully understand our personas in order to empower ourselves by having choice over how we act and respond.

Opening Up to the Shadow

Shadow behaviors and feelings usually developed from childhood experiences that were too painful to deal with, thereby locking in fear, anger, rage, deep sadness, or loneliness, feelings that remain hidden in our current lives. They may also have resulted from strong societal or religious messages of what is wrong and therefore unacceptable. Often they come from feelings or behaviors that had been disapproved of by our caretakers, either by ridicule and reprimand or by approval of the opposite behavior. We internalized these parental or societal attitudes and still carry them with us, continuing to repress or judge these aspects, behaviors, or feelings when they arise. When they do arise we often deny that they are really part of us.

Becoming aware of our shadows not only enables us to make more conscious choices in our lives, but also gives us the opportunity to more fully love ourselves. By sending love and acceptance to aspects of ourselves we have not approved of, we are allowing for more authenticity and greater creativity.

Once you access your willingness to uncover your shadows, you open a door to discovering more about them and gain more insight into these hidden aspects. You gain this insight by paying attention and noticing what you do in daily life—what you say on a regular basis, how you say it, how you respond to others, how they respond to you, and so forth. The shadow can be feelings, roles, or ways of being that you may know exist but have chosen to ignore. Or it might be feelings and aspects that are so totally unacceptable to you that until you begin to look for them you have absolutely no awareness of. As you become more aware of these shadow feelings or behaviors, part of the healing is to not judge them. Simply shining the light of your awareness on them often brings about change. Other times it is about consciously changing a behavior that you have come to realize is not fully serving you. Becoming a witness to yourself, doing the exercises in this book or writing about what you notice, will heighten your awareness and teach you more about yourself and your shadow.

Projections of the Shadow

We are often quick to ridicule others for traits or behaviors that in some way resemble aspects of ourselves, however repressed. In doing this we are projecting onto others what exists in us that we do not want to acknowledge. When we blame, hate, criticize, or reject someone for something that exists in ourselves, it is called *projection*, and paying attention to such behavior is a great way to discover what aspects of ourselves we have denied. However, *owning* our projections—discovering and claiming as true—can take a great deal of willingness and honesty.

The shadow can be either positive or negative traits. If the traits are positive, we may have chosen not to recognize them because we would then have to take responsibility for them, that is, stretch out of our comfort zone to incorporate those aspects into our lives. For example, for some people ambition may be considered a negative trait because over-ambition blocks their ability to feel or just be, while for others acting on one's ambition is a positive growth step and can be denied like any other trait. Mary, a housewife, was moderately comfortable, yet depressed and unfulfilled, working strictly in the home. She judged and ridiculed her sister, who had a highly successful and fulfilling career as an independent consultant. Eventually she accepted that she also had a desire for more worldly achievement. This had remained a shadow trait for a long time because focusing on this desire would mean making considerable changes in her life. Once her desire was owned and taken out of the realm of the shadow, she was able to face the changes and move forward toward her ambitions.

Another example of a positive shadow is our powerful expressive self. Have you ever noticed yourself either judging or idealizing some outrageous public figure? Chances are their ability to be seen or achieve what they want instills a reaction in you and you either criticize them or put them on a pedestal rather than try to achieve your own full potential. Until we are ready to grow, we will keep such aspects, whether positive or negative, hidden in the dark recesses of our consciousness and continue to project them onto others.

Self-Responsibility Versus Being the Victim— The Power of Owning Projections

When we blame our circumstances or other people for things we don't like in our lives, rather than accept responsibility by taking steps to change them, we are playing the victim. Some suggest that some things can't be changed, and individuals are not being victims in recognizing this. However, *victim consciousness* does not refer to being in situations that are unfavorable or where someone has been a victim of something, it is the consistent blaming and unwillingness to attempt to make changes where we can.

> *We also play the victim when we don't "own our projections," that is, when we don't see that what is happening to us in the outer world is actually mirroring our inner selves.*

The following story epitomizes victim consciousness. Jim, one of my patients when I was a chiropractor, was a street person, although he was not your average one. He was very intelligent, well read, generally clean, and had a heart of gold. Periodically I would take on charity cases, and I considered Jim to be one of them. To his credit Jim found an agency to pay for his treatment since he had too much pride to accept it for free. In the end, however, the agency did not pay so a year later Jim scraped enough money together and insisted on paying part of the bill himself. This behavior showed me that he had the inherent ingenuity and capability to change his circumstances if he chose to do so.

Jim had experienced the following things before I met him: he had been hit by a runaway truck as a pedestrian; he was an alcoholic; and six months earlier he had been violently pushed off a cliff. He was in enormous pain—both emotionally and physically—and was constantly nauseous, claiming he had vomited every day for the past several years. Although Jim was only thirty seven, he looked closer to sixty.

After a few weeks of our work together, Jim's physical condition improved. He could keep his food down, and his physical pain was lessening. Knowing that physical ills start as emotional states, I began to discuss life philosophy with him. Because he seemed receptive to what I was saying, I decided to give him a book that has changed many lives, *You Can Heal Your Life* by Louise Hay. The book teaches that on some level—consciously or unconsciously—we play a part in most everything that happens to us, no matter how horrible it may seem, for the purpose of learning and growth. It also suggests that there is a divine order of cause and effect in the universe, and what we believe deep down about ourselves and life will be reflected in our lives. According to this book, Jim couldn't blame anyone else for his misfortune, and ultimately he alone (with the help of a power greater than himself) could take actions to improve his situation. If he began looking at his own issues, beliefs, and actions rather than consistently blaming everything external to himself, ultimately life and others would support his efforts. He would be taking responsibility for his own life.

I was feeling proud that I might have helped change Jim's life. Since I had improved his physical condition, I believed I could also turn his thinking around so he could be truly healed. However, I was surprised and humbled when, after finishing the book, Jim came into my office raging mad, saying, "That book made me really angry!" He explained that he couldn't agree with any of it. He forced himself through it because he liked me and appreciated what I had done for him, but he was really upset.

Why did he get so mad? Because the book challenged all his beliefs. If he accepted what it said, it would invalidate the psychological ground on which he stood. Hearing ideas so different from his own, especially the idea that he had to start taking responsibility for his life, made him fearful, which he expressed as anger. Not realizing this at the time, I tried unsuccessfully to convince him of the truth in the book.

Finally, I realized that to best serve him I needed to let go of my need to change his thinking and ways. Consequently, I decided to give Jim as much love as possible and simply accept him for who he was—no more philosophizing or trying to convince him how much Alcoholics Anonymous would help him. I would just let him be and see the good in him. It is interesting that during the time I was most pressuring Jim to change, his physical condition took a backslide. When I released my attachment to changing him, he started to improve again. Unfortunately, this improvement didn't continue. Several years later, after Jim stopped treatment, my assistant who was working late one night reported that Jim came running in, saying, "Can I go hide in a room? They're chasing me!" Apparently a group of other like-minded individuals were throwing beer cans at the office window, with Jim as the object of their assault—the victim. Evidently, he had continued to avoid taking responsibility for his life and continued to be the victim.

Jim epitomized the philosophy by which many live their lives, to one degree or another—the belief that life is basically beyond our control and we are victims of circumstance, upbringing, race, nationality, economic status, or any other external factor.

Every time we blame or point the finger at others for what happens to us, we assume the role of victim and fail to take full responsibility for our lives. Conversely, to live a whole and balanced life that leads to the fullest expression and creativity, we need to embrace the philosophy of self-responsibility. According to this philosophy, not only do we create many of our current circumstances due to choices (often unconscious), we also have the power to release the old and create what we consciously desire, whether it is a loving relationship, worldly success, or inner peace. Because our deepest held beliefs and values have the power to attract certain types of people and circumstances to us, we can change our situations for the better by looking at our inner world, changing our beliefs, and taking new actions. (See Chapter 10 for further discussion of this topic.) It is not to say that along with being able to change and create circumstances, things sometimes don't also just happen at random. Although this may be true, we can either let them block us by feeling helpless and blaming life or others for those random circumstances or we can accept them and do what we can to make the best of it.

Self-responsibility encompasses the ability to drop all blame, accusations, judgments of others, or any other form of outward finger pointing and learning to turn the finger back at ourselves, that is, own our projections. This involves transforming the blame to a way of learning about ourselves. Taking responsibility means asking ourselves, "What is in this for me to see, feel, or learn about myself that would otherwise be impossible for me to learn?" Sometimes it is helpful to first identify the essence, or bottom line, of what it is others are doing to you that upsets you most before asking the previous question.

For example, Tom, a man I counseled, was very angry at his wife, Susan, who had been unfaithful for a number of years. When I saw him three years after this discovery, they had separated and were in the process of getting a divorce. He wanted the divorce and a new start, but there had been many delays in the court proceedings, and he was unable to get completely involved in a new relationship. Even though Susan desperately wanted to start fresh after she had admitted her infidelity, Tom couldn't find it in himself to forgive her. In order to identify the essence of his shadow and projection and hence the cause of his inability to forgive and let go of her, I asked him, "What about what she did makes you most angry?" He said the dishonesty. I then asked, "How are you also being dishonest in your life?" He was just starting on a path of self-awareness, and it was too big an act of self-responsibility for him to acknowledge that he was dishonest with himself in some way, so he kept saying that he was always honest. But it was clear to me that he was equally dishonest, just in a different way. He was a people pleaser who worried about others' opinions and consistently gave up his truth to defer to others' desires. Moreover, he worked in a corporate environment where he felt compelled to uphold a certain image but was actually a creative, adventure-loving, and artistic person holding back the truth of who he was from himself and others. Even though we think that dishonesty is only lying or cheating, omission is also a form of dishonesty. Withholding our truth is being dishonest with ourselves and others. The dishonesty Tom saw in his wife was an opportunity for him to look at his own dishonesty.

Over time Tom was able to see things in himself he had accused his wife of and own them. With this ownership, he was able to let go of his anger toward her. As he let go of the anger, he subsequently began to feel love for her again, and then his grief at the loss of his marriage. This allowed him to fully let go, and later he was able to be in a satisfying long-term relationship. How many relationships can we heal, current or old, by looking at what they reflect in us and thereby taking responsibility?

One of the wonderful benefits of this work is that by changing yourself you create the space for others to change as well. The old adage that we can't change anyone but ourselves is true. If you find yourself exceedingly frustrated by someone else's behavior because there is nothing you can do about it, rather than trying to coerce change in the other, which only makes matters worse, take solace in the fact that you can always work with yourself. Ask yourself, "What is it in the other person that is frustrating me (or making me angry) that has some counterpart in me, and what can I learn about myself from this?" Although it can be the exact same trait, most often it will be something similar with a different twist or a counterbalancing opposite trait. The process described in the following pages will give you the tools to discover useful insights in any difficult or frustrating situation.

Taking the focus for change off another person and placing it on yourself can have amazing results. When we blame, hold judgment toward someone, or anxiously want them to change, it is as if there is a force field of energy pushing against them, which only serves to keep them fixed in their position. As soon as we shift the focus and take the pressure off them by directing the attention back to ourselves, it gives them the energetic or psychic space in which to change or come forward. It is quite amazing to watch this happen. Many times when I have pulled back the blame and judgment, and assessed myself instead, a person in my life has magically changed their attitude. They don't even have to be present; one time I did this with someone who was 3,000 miles away. The night after I fully owned my projection, he miraculously called with an entirely different attitude and willingness to change his position. Further, a person doesn't even have to be alive for the healing or growth potential in that relationship to be realized for the person doing the work. I have seen healing and transformation occur consistently for myself and others who have integrated the practice of owning projections into their lives. In addition, as we change how we do the dance, we change the entire relationship dynamic, allowing others to respond to something different.

The story of the healing of my relationship to my former husband is a good example of how the work one person does can effect the other. I married a man who was a reflection of my extremely strong and active inner critic. Even years after the marriage, while we were still interacting frequently due to joint custody of our child, he continued to be extremely critical. This aspect of our relationship mystified me since I had been doing everything I knew possible to bring about a positive change.

Our healing process seemed to occur in four distinct stages. The first major shift occurred when I stood my ground on a very big issue that I would normally have altered my position on in order to gain approval. The second major shift happened when I began to acknowledge my own deep-rooted feelings of anger. I no longer blamed him for expressing his anger because I came to realize it was just a reflection of the anger I had been unaware of inside me. Though I never said anything to him about this, our relationship began to lighten up tremendously after I owned this projection. The third major shift occurred when I began to make peace with my own inner critic and no longer needed my former husband to reflect this aspect of myself. The final major shift began as I opened more to my vulnerability. As I became defenseless (stopped defending myself in the face of any accusations) and vulnerable to more of my feelings as well as his, the last barrier that kept us from being able to relate harmoniously finally lifted.

This story makes the point that we must let go of blame and judgment if we are ever to have peace in our relationships. By stopping the blame game and simply asking ourselves, "What is this reflecting in me and in what way do I need to change?" we accept responsibility for ourselves. This does not mean that others are innocent, and circumstances are all our fault, but every dynamic between two people involves 100 percent participation from each party. Both people bring their circumstances, histories, and shortcomings to the exchange. When we learn there is no "bad guy," only one who is expressing an aspect of an issue more obviously while the other is keeping an aspect of the issue hidden, we see that no one is to blame, and both are responsible. It is clear that the bottom line in any relationship dynamic involves facing our own issues. We may request a change or ask that our needs be met, but ultimately, whatever the response is, we must still be able to find peace in ourselves. Despite any major behavioral changes they make or we desire on their part, one way or another it is the changes in ourselves that matter the most. When we take responsibility for our part, and do our own work, the result is progress for ourselves and ultimately those close to us.

The following process, if approached with genuine willingness, can help you find the hidden shadow aspects of yourself and own your projection in any situation. When I use this process in my workshops, it is very common for people to have difficulty seeing that they harbor the same or similar behavior as those they accuse. This initial resistance can be overcome with perseverance. When it is, new doors open to expanded awareness and usually relationship breakthroughs. I will take you step by step through this process and give you some examples from our workshops, in order to help make it a little easier. I credit Gay and Kathlyn Hendricks, who wrote *Conscious Loving* and many other wonderful books, with the eloquent wording of some of these questions.[7]

Identifying and Owning Projections

The following questions will help you move out of blame and into a more empowered state. They are listed here with descriptive details and a more concise version is repeated in the Try It section without the explanations.

Step 1: Finding the essence of the projection.

1. Define the problem.

    "What do I see 'out there' (in the other person) that causes me pain, (aggravation, anger, sadness, and so forth) that if I opened up and got the lesson from (took responsibility for) would cease being a problem?"

2. In order to access the essence or bottom line of what someone is doing that upsets or disgusts you, fill in these blanks: "They are being too ___, or so ___ or not enough ___, or they are ___ing me."

3. Another way for getting to the essence is to ask the following question:

    "What aggravates me most about what (someone you are upset with) has done or is doing?"

Step 2: Getting the lesson—Finding what the projection has to show you.

Once we have identified the core or essence of the projection, the next step is to get the lesson. The following questions are helpful in this:

1. "How is this similar to an earlier time in my life?" Try going back to the earliest memory.

2. "How do I also ___ myself?" Complete the sentence with whatever you filled in for questions 2 and 3 above. Ask yourself how you do essentially the same thing to yourself or others, in perhaps a slightly different manner, or something different but with similar elements.

For instance, I was working with a woman who felt she had been ripped off in her business by a man who promised to sell her a particular grade of product, but who, after being paid in full, sent her a lower grade. I asked her what most aggravated her about this, and she said, "He lied to me—he didn't tell the truth." The next question was, "How do *you* also not tell the truth in your life?" As a result, she acknowledged how much she had been ignoring her own truth. She then realized it was essential for her to start paying attention to her feelings and be more honest with herself and others.

3. "Is this a call to balance an aspect of myself or my behaviors? If so, what is the aspect and what direction am I being called to move toward? In what area of my life does this aspect show up most?"

Sometimes the learning is about an aspect of you that is off in one direction and calling for some balance. Don't be misled by accusations you make that you believe have absolutely nothing to do with you, and in fact you believe you are quite the opposite. For example, a woman complained, "My husband is always picking on the way I do things. He tries to control what I do and put it in little boxes. He's too rigid." He complained, "She's so disorganized. She is too wild." This couple needed to learn from and integrate aspects of each other's behavior. A good question in this case is, "How can we meet each other half way?" For this woman, it was about learning to draw upon her own inner strength, set boundaries for herself, and learn more focus. For the man, it was about allowing himself to loosen up.

As you look for the lesson about a quality that appears to be the opposite of that exhibited by the person you are blaming, also look for some aspect in you that might be similar. If you look hard enough you should be able to find some way in which the trait is present in you as well, although it may be slightly altered. For example, Rich and Nicole were another pair of opposites. Rich was very unstructured and understood that he had Nicole in his life to teach him how to be more organized. But what seemed to awaken him the most was discovering how he was similar to Nicole. He had worked in his father's business since he was very young, and although he liked the lifestyle it provided, he was uninspired. Even though he said he was content, he appeared to be dissatisfied and unfulfilled. Whenever the subject of changing careers to something more meaningful came up, he quickly defended the virtues of making good money and having a few good vacations a year. After insisting that "no way in heaven" was he anything like Nicole, a light bulb finally went off, and he realized that just as he saw Nicole as rigid, he was rigidly holding onto this job and his belief in security, without being open to other possibilities. Although he thought he exemplified flexibility, he finally "owned" the rigidity that was characterized by Nicole and saw that he was not always different from her. This helped him to stop blaming her and come to terms with this aspect.

To find the lesson in the things we blame others for, we must be open and honest with ourselves since the answers are not always obvious. When we find the lesson, we know it since it usually has an uplifting and energizing effect. We get the "Ah-ha!" response.

Another example of looking for the subtleties to find the gem is illustrated by my work with a woman named Candice. She criticized her boyfriend for always "should-ing" on himself and others, that is, telling himself and others what they should do. She claimed she was not like that but could accept people and that she no longer talked to herself in critical ways. She did not believe that she was anything like her boyfriend. I brought to her attention that only moments earlier she had been telling me she had been upset with herself because she had fallen into an old pattern of behavior. Essentially she was saying "I should have done this differently" and was angry at herself even though she denied many times that she was telling herself she "should" do anything. A strong insistence that there is no reflection of ourselves in the behavior of others is a key sign that a hidden aspect may exist. When Candice saw that the implication of "should" in her feelings of anger around her behavior was essentially the same as saying the words to herself, she learned the lesson in the situation, which was that the "should-ing" she blamed her boyfriend for was still part of her own personality and required more attention. Seeing that what she blamed him for was also in her helped her to let go of her "charge" on his behavior.

4. "What can I learn about myself that would be impossible to learn any other way?"

We don't always have others to help us hold the mirror to ourselves when we lay blame or feel victimized. Rather than be supported in owning your projections, the general approach is to enlist team members on behalf of your victimhood—cohorts in how you have been done wrong or in blame slinging. Although it can be challenging, you are the one who can stop the conspiracy and break up the "blame team." If you can't seem to see the reflection or get the lesson, then just *hold the question*. Pick any one or two of the previous questions mentioned and hold it in your consciousness or repeat it a few times a day. With an open mind, eventually the answer will become clear, either in a life circumstance or as an intuitive awareness. When the lesson has truly been learned, that is, the blame has been stopped and the emotional charge has lifted, you will be complete with that particular issue.

Often the question arises about who should do the work to own a projection. In any relationship dynamic both people can find something to own. When both do this it can be very satisfying and brings about great intimacy. But in many cases there is one person who is upset and the other does not quite understand what they are so upset about. Though it is important to communicate what you are feeling in a non-attacking way and make a request for change with an openness that they may not respond to your request, it is equally important for the one who has the greatest "charge" to do the work to own the projection. It is this charge or upset that lets you know an issue is being triggered. It is one thing to say, "If they stop doing the thing they do, I will not have an issue," but the idea is to go deeper and discover why you consistently manifest someone who does this and triggers these feelings in you. Even if it looks like it is "all their fault" it is good to hold the question, "what is my part?" until an answer arises.

The higher aspect of your being is always attempting to move you forward. When you understand what your life circumstances are trying to show you and incorporate the learning into your life, it is no longer necessary to repeat the same circumstances. Then the need for this particular lesson, and thus the circumstances or behaviors that brought it to your attention, are diminished or eliminated. When you fully own your issues and take steps to change or balance them, you will have fully taken responsibility for the issue and will be freed from that particular dynamic. Sometimes this happens immediately, and other times it takes time for the lesson to be absorbed and reflected back in life changes. When we have fully owned our part in the creation of a circumstance, and have the desire to learn something about ourselves that assists in our evolution, we then open ourselves to a higher level of consciousness and creativity.

Step 3: Moving on in life

Once we have learned the lesson and are willing to move off of what doesn't work, then taking responsibility entails moving forward to create what we do want. The following question will help you move forward.

1. "What kind of teacher do I no longer require in my life?" In other words, what kind of teaching does the person you projected onto represent?

2. Officially fire the person or circumstance from the job of being teacher.

Now that you learned the intended lesson, you no longer need them to show you this. Make a verbal proclamation with intention that you are releasing this person from having to be a teacher of this lesson. You now understand what you must do to embrace what you learned about yourself. You can release this person from being a teacher without releasing him or her from your life, unless you want to.

3. "If I take full responsibility and see, feel, and learn what I am to learn in the situation, what creative potential does this release in me? In what positive way will I or my life be different?"

When asking ourselves the questions that assist us in getting the learning, particularly with a challenging circumstance, it is helpful to be inspired by where this lesson can ultimately take us.

4. "How will my life potentially look in one year, five years, 10 years, 20 years if I fully take responsibility in this issue."

Seeing the future cumulative effect will show the importance of taking care of this now.

Learning to own our projections is one of the most powerful tools for opening ourselves up to what is holding us back. It is a quick and effective way to access disowned and less than obvious aspects of our being. When these aspects are allowed to remain hidden, they sabotage our best efforts to move forward in our lives.

Have your attitudes, perceptions, and judgments of others or circumstances made you healthy, happy, and full of joy and peace? Or have you felt like a victim? Perhaps it is time to stop blaming others or circumstances for your situation and embrace self-responsibility by discovering, owning, and accepting your shadow aspects. Doing this consistently is an important step on the path to greater fulfillment and creativity.

TRY IT!

1 | Personas

☐ Look at the list of personas in this chapter. Write down any of these that you can relate to and any others not listed that may apply to you.

☐ To gain more insight into the origins, nature, and purpose of the persona, answer the following questions for each persona you've identified for yourself. These questions can be answered on a piece of paper, writing for the voice of the persona. This is best done with a friend asking you the questions as the persona or alone using the intuitive dialogue style—with a seat in front of you that you can move into as you answer the questions from the voice of the persona. When speaking as the persona, take on the physiology, that is, a position and voice quality that best represents the character. Credit to Gay and Kathlyn Hendricks[9] for this series of questions:

❏ "What is the most important thing to you?"

❏ "What are you most proud of?"

❏ "When did you make your first appearance?"

❏ "Who did you learn your style from?"

❏ "What are you most afraid of?"

❏ "What feelings are you trying to hide from?"

❏ "What are you trying to accomplish for me?"
Look for the positive intent.

❏ Direct the next questions toward yourself, the individual.
  ❏ "What limiting belief is this persona acting out?"
    For example, I have to perform to be lovable, or I have to have a problem to get attention.

  ❏ "What truths does this persona keep me from being aware of?"
    For example, the truth that who I am, without having to prove myself, is worthy.

  ❏ "What other complementary personas in others are necessary for this persona to operate?"
    "In other words, in order for me to play _____ (i.e., super competent), I must see _____ (my partner, co worker, etc.) as _____ (incompetent, helpless, etc.)."

  ❏ "Is there anything else I notice about this persona?"

  ❏ "What might occur if I loved and accepted this persona?" (If it is one you judge negatively.)

2 | Take responsibility for your life and actions.
❏ Make a list of the ways you see yourself as a victim of circumstances or other people.

❏ For each situation ask yourself the following questions and write your immediate responses.
  ❏ "What is attractive to me about this?"

  ❏ "What might be hidden motives for me to have this in my life?"

  ❏ "Is there a deeper issue here and what is it?"

  ❏ "What can I do now in my present circumstances that would begin to positively transform this situation?"

❑ List one or two possibilities, no matter how unattainable they seem, that would provide an alternative to the present circumstances.

❑ Make a commitment to yourself to take one action step or make one choice each day, however small, to change the circumstances in which you feel a victim.

3 | Owning projections and discovering a shadow aspect by taking responsibility for blame and accusations.

The following are the questions I discussed in this chapter. Select an issue and answer the questions, letting your most immediate response arise. If you get stuck on any question, refer to the explanations for each question in the chapter.

❑ **Accessing essential element**
   ❑ "What do I see out there that causes me pain or upset that if I opened up and got the lesson, would cease being a problem?"

   ❑ Fill in the blanks in regard to someone you have a complaint about:
   "They are too ___, so ___, not ___ enough, or they are ___ing me."

   ❑ "What aggravates me most about what they have done or are doing is ___."

❑ **Getting the lesson**
   ❑ "How is this similar to an earlier time in my life?" (Start with earliest possible circumstance.)

   ❑ "How am I also ___." (Referring to the answers from the questions above.)

   ❑ "Is this a call to balance an aspect of myself or my behaviors? If so, what is the aspect, and what direction am I being called to move toward?"

□ "What can I learn about myself that may have been impossible to learn any other way?"

□ **Moving on—moving forward**

☐ "What kind of teacher do I no longer require in my life?"

☐ "With a verbal proclamation, officially fire the person or circumstance from being a teacher of what you have learned."

☐ "If I take full responsibility and see, feel and learn what I am to learn in this situation, what creative potential does this release in me? In what positive way will I or my life be different?"

☐ "How will my life potentially look in one year, five years, 10 years, 20 years if I fully take responsibility for this issue?"

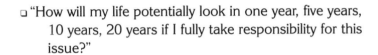

chapter eight
Disarming the Inner Critic

According to a common school of thought, a number of sub-personalities exist in our subconscious, such as the "inner child," "protector," and "controller." Though there are many more, these are some of the key players. Each one has a different set of values, desires, motives, and personality. If given the opportunity to speak its intentions for us, each one has a different voice. Giving each one acceptance, listening to its desires, and honoring its feelings will help soften its influence on us. Each of the sub-personalities has a potential negative influence on us, but just as any negative aspect of our personalities has a positive side, so do these characters. We need to transform each from nemesis to ally. This chapter discusses how this can be done by focusing on one key player—the inner critic.

The inner critic is that harsh and sly character that can attack us at every turn. It has an uncanny ability to hold us back from moving forward in a positive way, from being able to take risks, to love, have fun, or be creative. The inner critic's way of operating is different with each individual. Sometimes the words the critic uses are blatant reproaches easily noticed and counteracted; for example, you may say to yourself "that was stupid," or "you jerk." Other times the critic is more insidious, speaking to you in less obvious ways that can be harder to detect.

Once the habits of the inner critic are brought to your awareness, you can then make a practice of focusing your attention on these subtle voices to transform them.

Here is an example of how my inner critic worked its devastation. I had done a lot of self-examination, but it still felt like something was holding me back from living life fully. I felt as though a weight were dragging behind me—every step or two that I took forward, it pulled me back at least one. What was this mysterious thing that so clearly was dampening my initiatives, dulling my spirit, and lowering my energy level? By asking the question, "What is holding me back and how can I move through it?" I gained the awareness of what I was doing to myself. I noticed that I was constantly saying either out loud or to myself, "I shouldn't have done this," or "I should have done that." Thus, reminding myself of my mistakes many times a day. By itself, this doesn't seem so bad and could be understood as merely a reminder of what to do or not do next time. However, it is the attitude behind these remarks of the inner critic that is devastating to the inner child. In this case, the insinuation was, "You dummy, you can't do anything right." Such an accusation was a very low blow to me because at the time I still believed my value as a human being was directly related to my "doing" and my "doing right." No matter how much I worked to raise my self-esteem, my inner critic continuously undermined it by implying that I was stupid and couldn't do anything right. The results of this kind of treatment toward oneself can be devastating and cause one's inner child to rebel or shut down completely, leading to depression and health problems. This critical treatment also reduces the ability to try new and potentially risky things that might ultimately bring joy and fulfillment.

The awareness of this incessant "shouldn't" was a major breakthrough for me. Over time and with concentration, I was able to turn this voice around. Not only did it stop criticizing in its many subtle ways, but a new voice developed that was loving and supportive. I find it helpful to think of this process as transforming the critical inner parent into the nurturing parent.

A child thrives when parents are supportive and accepting of his or her behaviors and mistakes. By contrast the child will act out, misbehave, or withdraw when parents are condescending, unforgiving, and critical. The tone of voice is also important. As I became more aware of the critical way I spoke to myself, I noticed that I was speaking to my own daughter in a similar impatient, condescending manner. Although I had thought I was a loving parent, since I never directly said negative things to her, I eventually saw that there was a pervasive negative tone in my voice when she did things I didn't like. Further, her reaction to my voice caused some of her actions, to which I then responded negatively, creating a vicious cycle.

However, as I changed my internal voice, I was able to change the tone of voice with which I spoke to her, thereby improving our relationship dramatically.

The following is a list that illustrates some of the ways the inner critic operates. Its methods are many and unique to each individual. Use this list to gain awareness of the ways your own inner critic works.

- Tone of voice (authoritarian, denigrating, regretful) out loud or internally
- Negative judgment of others
- Dissatisfaction with ourselves regarding body, performance, actions, behaviors, appearance, and so forth.
- Complaining and noticing what's wrong with things—usually with a slight whine in the voice.
- Focusing on worst case scenarios or negative possibilities.
- Body tension
- Specific words (for example, "I blew it;" "That was dumb;" "Brilliant" (said sarcastically); "I can't;" "Shouldn't;" "I did it again;" "When will I ever learn?"

After a group in one of my workshops opened up to their critic, they shared how it spoke to them or operated, such as in the following ways:

Things it says

- You are not capable—can't do it good enough or right.
- You don't compare—comparing self to others.
- You are too spiritual to be angry.
- You should know better.
- You should be more enlightened.
- You should be a better ___ (i.e., mother, income earner.

Ways it operates

- Fear of making a decision.
- Unforgiving of choices made that didn't turn out well.
- Intolerance for making mistakes.
- Being hard on oneself for not doing things up to a high standard.
- Minimizing feelings (ignoring the fact or telling yourself you shouldn't feel angry, sad, or scared when you do)
- Guilt tripping

The inner critic has many opportunities to speak to us because we continually fall short of a prescribed ideal. When we are growing up we come to believe that if we acted or appeared in certain ways we would gain approval and therefore love. As a result, we soon developed what is called the "idealized self." Many parental and societal restrictions and expectations are attached to this idealized self that we carry into adulthood. Examples are: how we should look or dress, how much money we should make, what kind of car we should drive, what type of career we should have, how we should treat others, what kind of parent we should be, and how our body should function. Living by the rules associated with the idealized self creates an ongoing problem. Every time we fall short of the idealized self, we prove the inner critic correct, giving the critic more ammunition. And because we judge ourselves according to this idealized self-image, rather than our true self, we often fall short of expectations.

Transforming the Inner Critic

An active inner critic will shut down the communication between the inner being and the outer self. This communication breakdown is a significant reason why we are out of touch with our feelings and inner truth. Thus, transforming the inner critic is an important step toward knowing our inner truth and being able to express it.

One of the ways we can transform the inner critic is by transforming its language from that of the critical parent to the nurturing parent. This is accomplished by applying attention to notice this harsh inner voice, then consciously saying something different. You might say "cancel" to what was just said and replace it with something gentle and accepting. This is described in more detail in Chapters 4 and 6.

Another powerful tool is to transform your inner critic into your ally. The inner critic is trying to serve and protect us in the only way it knows how. However, it has a distorted way of helping us win love and approval by pushing us to be the idealized self or the self that will received attention, or in some cases help us to not be noticed. In order to transform the inner critic, the first step is to get in touch with it's intentions and payoffs. The *payoff* means some benefit the inner critic is attempting to attain, but that may not be positive for us in the long run. It is trying to keep us from hurting ourselves or from being hurt by others. For example, if you decide you want to take a new direction in your career, and your critic has pointed out what is wrong with this option or that you are not good enough, the payoff may be that you don't have to risk failure. Such behavior seems positive to the inner critic, but to you it is not, because if you never take the risks that could result in failure, you will also never have the opportunity to create something truly fulfilling. You can usually find some way in which the inner critic thinks it is looking out for your best interests—this is finding the payoff.

The next step in transforming the critic into an ally is to focus on the more constructive aspect of the critic—the critics ability to discriminate between what is harmful for us and what is good. This involves consulting with this discriminator/advisor aspect of the critic whenever circumstances require a decision or good judgment, thus recognizing the value of the critic. Rather than saying, "The critic is bad; it causes me problems," which relegates it to the world of the disowned and unloved parts of ourselves, we can see it in a positive light, thereby integrating it.

An important aspect of the work of the path of truth is giving love and acceptance to every part of ourselves, including the part that judges things as unacceptable. In so doing, we begin to love ourselves fully. It's not, "Well, I'll love myself when I do a certain thing, or become or behave a certain way." It's loving ourselves in our entirety, right now— as is. Of course, this doesn't mean accepting all our behaviors but rather loving all parts of ourselves that are responsible for those behaviors. In conscious child rearing, it is considered "separating the child from the behavior" rather than condemning the child along with disapproval of the behavior. When doing this for ourselves, we must learn to put limits on certain behavior while still honoring the aspect of our being that is instigating the behavior. Seeing the critic as our discriminator and respecting it enough to consult it is a way to do this. When we can see the critic in its most positive light as discriminator and call upon it, we have taken an aspect of ourselves that has been actively holding us back and turned it into a supportive ally. We are able to use the critic's energy constructively rather than destructively and to motivate rather than inhibit.

Making peace with the inner critic by turning it into our ally is an important step toward internal peace. As you make peace with the inner critic, you will find there is no longer a need for others to reflect this conflict back to you. Thus people who are critical of you become less prevalent or shift themselves.

Susan, from one of my workshops reports: "I had an extremely challenging and uncomfortable relationship with my mother my entire life. Something absolutely amazing happened when I came to know and then make peace with my inner critic. My relationship with my mother magically shifted. Now we have a wonderful time together and love and enjoy each other very much."

My experience was similar to Susan's. When I finally owned, honored, and transformed my inner critic, my former husband stopped speaking to me in a critical tone of voice. Though there were other aspects to our healing, it was no longer necessary for him to reflect this critical aspect back to me.

Becoming aware of the inner critic's language, focusing your intent on softening it, and seeing the critic as an ally instead of a foe are important tools in transforming the inner critic. In addition, many of the other practices in this book will help transform the critic and its harsh effect, since positive practices support and build on each other. For example, the practice of listening to our inner self and honoring what is real for us, as opposed to a false ideal, will provide less ammunition for the inner critic. Moreover, the transformation of the inner critic will support the inner being in communicating what is true for it by creating a safe environment. All the practices work hand-in-hand and create an upward, spiraling effect.

Transforming the Critic—A Personal Story

I have talked about the inner critic's voice and the need to consciously change its language so that our inner being does not feel abused by the words, inferences or tones of voice. However, sometimes the critic isn't obvious in its expression and can make you feel wrong without even a word. Instead you may have an all-pervasive unsettling feeling that you don't understand unless you take the time to feel your feelings and inquire about the source. The following personal story illustrates how insidious the inner critic was for me.

It was a time in my life when I had committed to taking time for myself—to be, feel, and open to creative guidance. I wasn't generating a steady income and was willing to live off savings. My finances were precarious for some time because I hadn't yet received the internal message that it was time to move forward toward a particular goal. This way of living, already challenging enough, was made worse by my internal judgment. My inner critic constantly judged me because I was going against society's wisdom regarding finances—that it's foolish to just whittle away chunks of money rather than to invest it so it can grow.

During this time my father died and left me some money. As a result, I was challenged even more about this issue, because now it wasn't just society's message I was going against. I was directly opposing my father's beliefs about finances and in addition was now spending his money! While meditating, various discomforting feelings would arise—sometimes anger, other times sadness or hurt. A general feeling of ill ease pervaded daily, although I didn't understand what was going on since nothing in my external life seemed to be upsetting me—except that every time I wrote a check transferring money from my savings account into my checking account I would become angry or upset.

I decided it was time to access what I was feeling on a deeper level and clear the energy that caused me such discontent. So I wrote to myself, asking what I was really feeling. What came through was a feeling of shame—that I was bad because I was acting contrary to my strong beliefs about work and money. My strong inner critical parent was letting me know how wrong I was behaving through a general feeling rather than words. When I failed to live up to my idealized self concerning money, my inner critic reprimanded me with feelings of shame. While I was honoring my inner guidance to leave the time open, I was being attacked for crossing a conflicting value.

By writing to my inner self, I not only clarified what I was feeling but also gained an understanding about deep beliefs I held that affected the situation. I also discovered new beliefs that I could work with to supplant the old ones.

The old beliefs were:
  • I only deserve to make money when I am working hard, and especially under stress.

- Not working at producing worldly things is being lazy and very bad.
- My value as a human is equal to what I produce.

The new beliefs are:
- I can, deserve to, and am making money easily, even and especially while peacefully doing what I love. I can be peacefully productive.
- Quietness as well as doing what I love is nurturing for the soul and can ultimately result in abundance.
- Taking care of myself and my soul is equally as valuable and honorable as productivity or taking care of outer world things.

As I allowed myself to be with my feelings, honored the inner critic's voice, and practiced the replacement of negative beliefs with positive ones, I began to feel free from the negativity that had engulfed me. By becoming aware of my inner critic's judgments, I was able to release myself from its hold. I became able to do what I knew was right for me without the overbearing burden of the inner critic's energy weighing me down. Every time we unhook one more tentacle of the inner critic's grasp, we are that much lighter and freer to be who we are and do what is really right for us.

After this period of letting go of the safety of work and allowing myself the time to feel and work through many issues and programs, the pieces started falling into place for work that was creative and meaningful to me. I connected with the right people and after much hard yet fun work, we created a successful workshop/retreat business that offered people week-long transformational experiences in several beautiful locations. I had gone from doing work that felt abrasive to my soul to work that synthesized many of my talents and interests.

This story demonstrates how oppressive the inner critic can be and yet at the same time helpful in uncovering important limiting beliefs. Clearly, my inner critic helped me discover more about myself when I took the time and focus to look. Once these viewpoints were out in the open, I was able to choose what I wanted to keep, discard what I didn't and change the way I talked to myself. Rather than disown the inner critic, I simply disarmed it.

TRY IT!

The following is a powerful series of exercises used in the Quantum Shift retreats. When done with willingness, openness, and intent, they can have a lasting effect by transforming the inner critic to a supportive ally. Although these exercises can be done alone, it is supportive to do them with a friend or friends who can be working along simultaneously with you on their critic.

Transforming Your Inner Critic

1 | Write answers to the following questions spontaneously, trying not to censor your answers.
   ❑ "What are all the things you think are wrong with your body?"

   ❑ "What are all the things you should or shouldn't be or be doing?"

   ❑ "How are you not good enough?"

2 | Complete the following sentences (can be personal as in, "you are ___," or universal as in, "people are or do ___, life is ___."):
   ❑ "What my mother always said or implied to me was ___."

   ❑ "What my father always said or implied to me was ___."

   ❑ "When growing up, I was always expected to do or be ___."

   ❑ "Societal or parental programming that I have taken on that doesn't feel good to me is ___."

3 | Complete the following sentences (which have been adapted from Nathaniel Branden's tapes on self esteem[8]):
   ❑ "It is not easy for me to be self accepting when I ___."

❑ "One of my emotions I have trouble accepting is ___."

❑ "One of my actions I have trouble accepting is ___."

❑ "One of the thoughts I tend to push out of my mind is ___."

❑ "One of the things about my body I have trouble accepting is ___."

❑ "I like myself least when I ___."

❑ "Mother gave me a view of myself as ___."

❑ "Father gave me a view of myself as ___."

❑ "What I get out of disliking parts of myself or my behavior is ___."

❑ "Sometimes I use self blame to ___."

❑ "The scary thing about liking or accepting myself fully even with my faults is ___."

❑ "I am becoming aware that ___."

4 | Keeping in mind how the inner critic operates, via words, feelings, or attitudes, write the following question at the top of a page:
❑ "How does the inner critic speak to me or operate in my life?"

Write your first impression without judgment, either in whole sentences or simple remarks, (for example, "you jerk," "stupid," "feeling undeserving of good things"). Be open to subtle possibilities as well as obvious ones.

5 | Let yourself feel (be with) how you are feeling after having answered questions 1-4. Then put on some drum music or other fast rhythmic music and let yourself move and vibrate to the

rhythm. As you do this, think about all the "shoulds" in your life you would like to let go of (answers to 1 and 2). Do some throwing-off gestures with your arms and legs with the intention of releasing the energy of all this pressure to fit a pre-scribed ideal.

6 | Find a comfortable spot to sit, put a pillow or chair in front of you, and have a conversation with your inner critic by moving back and forth between your seat and the seat in front of you. When you sit in the inner critic's seat, it is helpful to assume a posture appropriate to the critic. Also let your voice take on the characteristic tone of the critic. Although this conversation can take the form of an internal dialogue, it is much more effective done out loud.

You—Speaking as yourself, ask your inner critic the following question:
"What purpose have you been trying to serve in my life?"
In other words, what is the "payoff?"

Critic—Move to the inner critic's seat and let the critic respond. You may go back and forth a few times having a conversation.

You—After the critic has answered your questions, move back to original seat and express the following:
  ❑ Genuinely thank the critic for trying to help you.
  ❑ Express your forgiveness and gratitude for its efforts on your behalf.
  ❑ Imagine what your critic might look like or a symbol for the critic.
  ❑ Imagine a door in front of you and the image of your critic is walking out through the door, (either walking through an open door or disolving through a closed one).
  ❑ Visualize the door turning into a glow of light and through that light, visualize another image walking toward you—the critic transformed into "the discriminator."

- As this image comes forward, experience it saying that it is here to serve you, to show you what is or isn't in your best interest.
- Embrace it and feel it's gentleness, strength, and love.
- Now ask the discriminator (the critic transformed) the following:
    - "Would you be willing to be my ally, to assist me and advise me, using only kind words?"
    - "How can you motivate me, in a way that is supportive and kind, to do the things that are good for me and avoid doing things that don't serve me?"
    - "Tell me about the new way you intend to operate in my life."

Discriminator—Move into the discriminator's seat and answer.

You—Return to your seat, thank the discriminator, and close your eyes for a closing visualization to anchor the new behavior.
- Imagine a situation where the critic might have criticized you in the past.
- Hear it say, "Oh yes, I remember we are doing things differently now."
- Hear a voice that inspires you and is your inner support even when things are difficult.
- Imagine another situation where the critic/discriminator says no to what is destructive for you and yes to what is good.

In doing these exercises, you will experience a transformation of your inner critic. Afterwards, be understanding with your inner critic when it sometimes forgets to behave the new way. If you hear the old voice, just gently remind it of the new behavior; over time the old voice and style of operating will rarely occur.

nine Moving Emotional Energy

We have spoken about stored emotions and their negative effects on our bodies and lives. But how do we safely unleash such emotions without creating a destructive volcano that could do harm to ourselves and others? Many people I have worked with at first said they were afraid to feel what was really there because of what might happen if they tapped into it. In my experience, however, I have never seen this be a problem. To begin with, when approached consciously, as when we intentionally seek to grow, the inner being will naturally let out only as much emotion as the individual can handle. In addition, releasing stored emotions is a step-by-step process that occurs in safe and constructive ways.

Sometimes getting these emotions out can be an involved process because the old feelings and emotions are energetically dense and gluelike. Consequently, sometimes they don't release quickly, even when we want them to. In addition, the inner child is the keeper of the gate and needs to feel safe enough to let them out. Further, to have your inner child feel safe we need to be in a safe environment—a familiar or comfortable place where there will there be no interruptions. More importantly, the inner child has to feel a sense of trust and safety with you. It's an upward spiraling effect. As you practice accepting your day-to-day feelings without censorship, judgment, or rationalization, accepting yourself fully, including your body, actions, words, or mistakes, and incorporating some of the other practices for actively loving yourself, your inner child will begin to trust you more and more. Although letting old, pent-up emotions out feels risky to your inner child, it becomes more willing to take this risk as you build a relationship of trust.

The best way to begin releasing emotions stored in the cellular memory is through the body itself—either passively or actively, or preferably by both means. Passive approaches include deep tissue massage, certain forms of Chiropractic, Rolfing, Jin Shin, or any other therapeutic body work. An active approach is any practice that moves and releases energy with active participation by you. My experience shows consistently that active methods are essential and that passive ones support the process. When you take responsibility for your own healing by playing an active role in releasing energy, the result is much more effective and permanent. When working actively, it is helpful to have outside support such as a group, workshop, or therapist. You can use these outside resources to get you started, at key points along the way, or to support you throughout the process.

In this chapter I will share a number of my personal stories as examples of working with emotional release. My intention behind these experiences was to release stored energy and become clearer about what I was feeling in the present. Although some of the examples may seem more active than you might be comfortable with, any level of involvement will aid your ability to know and express your truth and release your creative potential. At the end of the chapter are a number of exercises that range from gentle to vigorous.

When you begin the journey of exploring your emotions it is helpful to start by asking your inner child if it would be willing to share its feelings. Although it may not be ready at that time, if you continue the practices to regain your inner child's trust, it will eventually agree to share its feelings. Accessing your inner child's willingness to begin this exploration is essential to the process. If you force that vulnerable part of yourself to feel things it doesn't want to, you could shut down more. Your willingness to accept whatever comes up, however large or small, is an important part of the process.

I experienced this during a week-long workshop where the focus was accessing core emotions through the body. Some of the processes we used for bypassing the mental defenses were breathwork and body-centered therapy. One of the things I got in touch with was how my inner child wanted to be left alone, huddled in the corner of her room (in my subconscious). As she began to speak to me, it became more clear that she was huddled in that room because she was tired of always being told what to do and how to do it. In the past, I had been a hard driver, often making myself do things that I really didn't want to do, not only to help others and survive financially but also for the sake of growing and stretching. Although such stretching is good to a point, rarely taking the feelings of my inner child into consideration made her feel pushed. As a result, my inner child shut down. I realized that my work entailed honoring her and allowing her to just be. This was an act of giving her my complete acceptance.

Taking an attitude of surrender in this workshop wasn't easy for me because I was there to let go of the past's hold on my body and being. Nevertheless, as others were powerfully releasing and nothing was coming up for me, I kept loving and nurturing my inner child by letting her know that whatever she wanted to show me would be OK, even if she just felt like staying quietly in her room. Throughout the week I reminded her that she didn't have to do anything other than just be. Although the workshop ended without any monumental experiences, I was content in knowing that I had successfully accepted my inner being in a situation where previously I would have disapproved of her performance.

An interesting thing happened after the workshop was over. As my inner child was feeling safe with me and beginning to trust that I would be there for her no matter what, she opened up and expressed herself in a way that she never had before. I suddenly found myself in a situation where many emotions were triggered—hurt, frustration, and anger—and was able to transfer these feelings, related to the current situation, to deep emotions that related to the past. As a result, while I was driving down the freeway, I had a release of anger and voiced sounds that came from the deepest core of my being. The release that I had hoped to experience in the workshop finally occurred when I was not forcing it. I took the initiative by going to the workshop and declaring the intention to explore and except my deeper feelings. She eventually trusted me enough to respond and opened in her own time. Although all this expressing may sound a little intimidating, over time you will develop the skills of *the observer*—the still part of you that knows you are not these feelings or this body. The observer can be watching calmly in the midst of great emotional expression.

Sometimes I feel my observer cheering me on, saying, "Right on, right on!" while I'm fully feeling and releasing some old emotion. While I was driving down the freeway yelling with an intense voice that came from deep down in my belly, another part of me was pleased and calm about what was occurring.

In Chapter 2, I discussed awareness as one of the first steps on the journey of creatively expressing yourself. Cultivating awareness can permeate every aspect of your life. You will learn to pay attention to the motivation for what you do and say, to notice patterns of behavior, and to watch yourself act out in emotional response to a situation. As you cultivate your inner observer and develop the capacity for awareness, you begin to experience a distancing from things you may have previously been identified with. The beauty of practicing self-awareness and cultivating the inner observer while working with emotions is that no matter how much stored emotion you tap into, you never take yourself too seriously. You know you are safe to feel these emotions, release the hold they have had on you, and then move through them to a new, more empowered place.

To access these buried feelings, a method that helps is the *active transference release*. Whenever feelings of irritation or anger come up, though they may not appear to have anything to do with feelings from the past, the energy in the present moment can be used to take you closer to where the deeper emotions are stored. When your emotions are triggered by another person or situation, if you pay attention you will notice that in addition to the pure emotion, you will be telling yourself things about the situation or people involved such as, "He never gives me any affection," "He is such a two-timing liar," or "She doesn't ever listen to me." At that point, ask yourself how this situation is similar to something from the past. Optimally, look for the earliest and first experience in what might be a chain of similar situations. Now consciously change the focus of your internal dialogue to regard the past event or go back and forth between the current situation and the past. As you shift your focus to the earlier event, let yourself fully experience your feelings and move the energy (described later in the chapter). You will free up energy from the stored emotions rather than only emotions related to the current situation. When you are in an emotional state regarding a current experience and you focus on a similar past experience, it is not uncommon for a new wave of emotion to emerge that is much bigger than the current situation alone would have triggered. When that happens, you know you are working with old material.

The following story is about a time when I was actively focusing on releasing old stored emotions. I had just received a disturbing phone call from my former husband. Although I was very calm during the phone call, he was sufficiently upset that he hung up on me. My first response was my usual reaction, to say, "How sad, he has such a problem," and proceed to blame him for various things, all the while maintaining my repose. Normally I would have continued my daily activities, feeling a bit off, but overlooking it one way or another. But this time I noticed that I had a strong, uncomfortable feeling in my chest and belly. I realized I could just sit on these feelings, as I often did, because I thought it was the noble response, or I could work with this energy. I chose to go to my room and started beating the bed with my fists and a pillow while letting out loud sounds. At first this reaction seemed contrived, but there came a point where I tapped into something. At that point I wasn't moving my body—my body was moving me. This shift point where we tap into the reservoir of emotion is called the *ignition point*. I understood that my upset concerning this situation was not just about what was happening now but was a replication of things that had happened in my past. With this understanding, I shifted my thoughts to a similar situation in my childhood and the people involved, and with this the emotion intensified. At this point I was releasing emotion from the past as well as the present. Under normal circumstances I might not have felt any upset at all thinking about the past, but the heat of the moment and the similarity to past feelings were enough to trigger stored, built-up emotion.

After the first episode of consciously working with my anger, I considered it a blessing anytime something made me angry or sad, because it was an opportunity to let go of one more layer of what held me back from my fullness. I discovered that I could use the upset I was currently feeling to assist the release of much deeper feelings. I did this by moving my body in various ways. Releasing the energy physically is called *moving the energy* and can take the form of shaking your arms and legs, stomping, kicking, hitting pillows, punching the air with fists, or bending over and shaking your head and arms while letting out loud uncensored sounds or growls. If the location prohibits loud noise, screaming into your hands can be effective, and under water screaming is also a fantastic release.

The practice of moving emotional energy can go beyond letting go of old feelings, it can also discharge current emotional energy that comes up in daily life. Since under most circumstances it is inappropriate to attack others with our anger or upset, releasing energy this way allows us to discharge the intensity of the built-up emotion. After we have released intense emotions, we are in a much better state of mind to communicate our true feelings compassionately and effectively, increasing the odds of finding a peaceful resolution to a problem.

For example, while on a long drive with a friend, I felt increasingly angry and hurt. It wasn't appropriate to direct the anger at him, so I stopped, went into an empty public restroom, and screamed into my hands while stomping my feet. When I came out, I felt more centered and was able to calmly communicate what I was feeling.

This kind of release can quickly bring you back to balance whether the emotion has been triggered by a person or a circumstance. Once I received some upsetting news regarding a project that I already had been quite upset about due to numerous delays. For months I had managed to stay calm every time I heard of another delay, rationalizing my feelings of upset by saying, "This is just a test of surrender," which it may have been. When I heard the news this time, I finally let myself go wild (move the energy) for a few minutes. Then I calmly went back to what I was doing from a true state of peacefulness rather than a contrived one.

If you are using this tool of emotional release as a way of dealing with some of your daily emotions as well as a method to clear the old repressed feelings, you will find that eventually there comes a point where the stored energy from the past will dissipate. After that fewer circumstances trigger you, you are less easily brought to upset and when you are, you can move off the feelings more quickly.

Although my examples of release relate to anger, release can occur with any emotion. The "being with" process at the end of this chapter is helpful for sadness or grief as well. This kind of work is often done in the context of a workshop or with a private therapist who specializes in emotional release work. However, doing emotional release work on my own has been such a powerful tool on my own journey that I propose it as a possibility for you as well. Many people hamper their growth because they are uncomfortable about working with others or because they can't afford it. Though I feel it is best to have outside support, working on your own can also be highly effective. It just takes willingness to get started. Once you see how powerful emotional release work is in restoring balance when you feel "off" or for bringing up and releasing old feelings, you will soon be motivated to use this tool.

TRY IT!

Although all the following exercises can be done alone, they are even more powerful and effective when done with another person or a small group. Often when our process is "witnessed" by another the healing is increased. In addition the group energy tends to intensify and speed up the process.

1 | Getting the Energy Moving

Here are three powerful exercises for moving, loosening up, and beginning to release stored emotional energy in the body. These exercises can also be used to move energy regarding daily emotions or just to keep you energized. They also serve as an effective warm up for the exercises that follow.

❑ To drum music, move and shake your entire body. It is especially important to rock your pelvis back and forth as the entire pelvic region, including the abdomen, houses a large percentage of the blocked energy. Do not be concerned if certain areas don't move as freely as others—in time they will.

❑ While moving and shaking the body, or even while sitting still, make sustained vowel sounds such as Ahhh -AAAA -EEEE -OOOH -UUUU. If you feel emotionally charged about something, it is particularly effective to release the charge through these sounds. Whether feeling emotions or not, making sustained vowel sounds has a discharging, healing effect on each of the energy centers of the body. If you are feeling tired or stressed, ten minutes of vowel sounding can completely alter your mood. Driving is a great time to practice sounding, though it is best if you can move.

❑ Lie down on your back with your knees up. Take a full breath in through relaxed lips and fill your diaphragm until your abdomen is puffed out. As you breathe in, let your pelvis rock forward, rocking the pubic bone toward the floor. Let the air come in as low in your pelvic cavity as you can—think of filling all the way to your pubic bone. As you let the air out, let your abdomen flatten toward the floor and the pubic bone rock up toward the ceiling as the air releases through relaxed, open lips. As you breath in again your pubic bone will tip down and your back will arch slightly. Let there be a smooth transition between the in-flow and the out-flow, with both the breath and the rocking of the pelvis. Do this for five to ten minutes.

❑ When the environment prohibits making much noise, you can yell or scream into your hands or pillow and if possible stomp your feet. You can also yell in the car. This practice of making loud sounds is good to do when something is first beginning to upset you.

These four practices—shaking or freely moving the body with pelvic movement, vowel sounding, pelvic breathing, and yelling, not only loosen up layers of dense energy from around and within the body, but also begin to release old layers of emotions held firm in the deeper recesses of the body. Do these exercises for a while before working with the next exercises.

2 | Being With and Emotional Release Exercises

❑ Body Centered Therapy—Being With Exercise[9]

This exercise assists "being with" an emotion. In order to release the energy of an emotion, you need to allow its presence to fully be with you. You can use this exercise to more fully experience what may only be a vague feeling, often resulting in greater relaxation and centeredness. Or it can be a prelude to fully moving and releasing the energy—active full-body release or the extended version at the end of this section. This exercise is a shortened version for everyday use. The extended version is best done when there is a lot of emotion already surfacing and you can take more time with the process.

When you notice that a feeling or emotion is starting to surface, close your eyes and ask yourself, "Where am I feeling this in my body?"

When you get the location—such as your chest, belly, throat, or shoulder—describe the qualities of the sensation in as much detail as possible (size, texture, color, density, and so forth). Both the location and the qualities may seem nebulous at first, but the more you focus your attention on them, the clearer these vague sensations become.

Once you have a sense of this, begin moving your body in a way that matches or describes the feeling or sensation. It is helpful to start with your hands out in front of you. Paint the qualities with your hands in the air, or let your hands move in a way that matches the feeling. Then let the movement extend into your entire body.

Next, exaggerate the direction that this is taking you. For example, if it's taking you into a ball, then continue into a very tight ball. If it's making jerky, staccato movements, exaggerate that with all your limbs by making even tenser, stiff-like movements. Use your entire body to express the feeling or sensation.

Now let out sounds that represent the feeling or emotion. This sounding can evolve into more vigorous ways of moving the energy such as stomping, punching pillows, or kicking and punching the air. Sometime during this process, you may hit the *ignition point* where you shift from acting out the emotion through your body to deeply feeling and uninhibited expressing. Often being with your current feelings will naturally transition into a release of older blocked emotions. Expressing feelings through your body allows them to naturally dissipate and transform. You have not blocked them, made them wrong or resisted them in any way. You have given them time and space to flow all the way through, which will leave you feeling peaceful and centered.

❑ Active Full Body Release Technique

Lie on your back on a bed or other soft surface, close your eyes, scan your body, and notice where you are feeling the most sensations in your body. Is there a heavy feeling in the belly? a constriction in the chest? and so forth. These sensations may be very subtle or strong and obvious. Focus on as many details about them as possible. (See the Being With Exercise from above.)

Once you have focused on the details in terms of either sensations or visual imagery, imagine this energetic form to be an independent entity. Now ask this form, which represents your emotion and that part of yourself that holds the emotion, what it wants to say. When you access it, the answer will usually be short—just a few words—whereas when you come from your more rational mind, the answer will be involved. You simply want to access key words—words that trigger and enhance the emotion, such as, "Leave me alone," "Get off my case," "I hate you," "It's not fair." Trust and go with whatever comes up. Say these words with a strong emphatic tone, kick the bed with your feet, and simultaneously pound with your fists. You can continue this until you are exhausted or feel complete. If you hit the ignition point where you begin to move more wildly, the energy will dissipate naturally.

To heighten the power of the release, stand up and take a tennis racket, baseball bat, towel with a knot tied at one end, "bataka bat" (soft bat made for this purpose), or any other firm object, and hit the bed as hard as you can with the object while repeating the key words. (Hitting the bed or pillow with your fists while upright or striking the bed with the pillow is an alternative.) The key words may change as you proceed, and allowing yourself to use foul language without judgment can be helpful.

❑ Active Transference Release

If the emotions were triggered by a current situation, rather than the bubbling up of old feelings, you can use the energy of this current situation to take you to your past. At some point in the middle of the release, ask yourself, "What is this similar to from my past?" Optimally, you will want to access the earliest possible occurrence, since most later occurrences are simply repetitions of the first, most deeply anchored one. Focus on this earlier circumstance as you repeat the key words and hit the bed. This will discharge and release the older stored energy. (See page 114 for more details.)

2 | Other Options for Emotional Release
❏ Creative Release

Creative expression of any sort is fun and fulfilling to the soul, not only because of what you create but because emotions are expressed and released in the process. If you are angry, try putting on powerful music and dancing with passion, beating a drum, writing extemporaneously, painting what you are feeling with intense colors or wild strokes, or singing with or without words to express what you are feeling. In this exercise you do not have to live up to any standard. Writing does not have to be logical, and drumming can be nonrythmic. Songs do not have to sound like anything you have ever heard before, and the singing can include growls and strange sounds or be beautiful and melodic. Just let it flow. There are no rules, it is about letting the emotion express through your creation. Such mediums, which can be used to express any emotion, including sadness, loneliness, or grief, use the body to varying degrees, yet are all effective in releasing the emotion.

❏ Meditative Release

When it is not possible to find the appropriate space for moving the energy physically, you can sit with your eyes closed and imagine you are moving and releasing energy with your body. For example, if you are feeling angry, visualize yourself going wild with your body and doing or saying anything that comes to mind. One time I did this I saw myself as a huge Godzilla-like creature stomping out entire cities. Do not judge this imagined behavior, but give yourself absolute permission to be as extreme as you like.

Another powerful option is to join visualization and prayer. Ask sincerely that the energy from the anger, grief, or whatever you are feeling be taken to the center of the earth and transformed to something equally powerful yet positive. Then imagine a stream of energy (red if it is anger) going from you into the earth and a golden stream coming back out and up into you. Every time I have done this, something amazing has happened later. Various emotions are just forms of energy, and like any other more physical forms of energy such as solids and liquids, they can be transformed.

❏ Physical Exercise With Intention

Most people understand that standard forms of exercise such as running, biking, hiking, or working out will dissipate negative emotions. Unfortunately, if we exercise simply to forget our problems, the emotions end up being repressed. Although some of the energy will get transformed so that you may feel better momentarily, the actual energy of the emotion will often just be pushed below the surface. You can use exercise, however, as an actual emotional release technique through conscious intention.

While engaging in the particular exercise, be thinking about what is triggering the emotional charge and integrate into your exercise a way to release this charge. Throw your arms and or legs out in a forceful way, or if this is impossible (such as when riding a bike), simply exert more energy than usual. Add to this some kind of releasing sound, such as growling or yelling. As you are moving in this more intense way and making sounds, visualize or hold the intention to discharge the energy around the issue. If possible, play music with a similar emotional content to accompany your exercise.

❏ Vocal Release

An easy technique that can be used with daily frustrations is simply to yell very loud. There are a number of ways this can be done without disturbing others, such as screaming underwater. When you feel tension build in your body and being, put your head underwater in the tub, hot tub, pool, or ocean, and yell. Other options are screaming in the car, or into your hands or pillow. If you scream long and hard, you may become hoarse, although if you hit the "ignition point," where you tap into your reservoir of emotions, you can yell as hard as you like, and it doesn't seem to affect the vocal chords. Such a release comes from such a deep place within that the vocal chords naturally relax, and the sound quality often changes as well. However, if you don't reach the ignition point, do not be concerned because release will still occur.

4 | Emotional Release—Extended Version

This process is most effective if some strong emotions around an issue are surfacing already. I have assisted many people through this process, although I have also instructed others to do it on their own. It can be highly effective done alone if you are willing to be with what you are feeling, though it is best if you have someone you trust who can support you. It is important that this support person stay centered as you access your emotions and not try to make you feel better, fix your problems, or talk you out of what you are feeling. They are simply there to witness and hold all your feelings as valid. They can ask the questions that are part of this process and should give you plenty of time between questions so you can take your time with the response.

Although not entirely necessary, music can greatly enhance the process. If you are experiencing hurt or sadness, find music with pathos in it or sweet gentle music. If you are feeling angry, some intense music will be best. Sometimes it is appropriate to have it on from the beginning, while other times it can be played as the feelings intensify. It is best to use a CD player and put the particular cut on repeat. Have plenty of pillows around and perhaps a cozy blanket.

The participants in this exercise will be:

Interviewer—the person asking the questions, either yourself if you are moving back and forth between roles or, optimally, another person.

Subject—you

Inner being—the inner child or whatever part of you is holding the emotion, i.e., angry child, powerful woman, lonely one etc. When in doubt, the inner child is best.

Nurturing parent—the gentle, loving part of yourself that can approach your inner being with kindness and acceptance.

Lie down on your back and get comfortable. Begin to breathe deeply, especially into your belly and pelvic region. Let your mind clear and your breathing relax and be fluid, being careful not to hold your breath. Then start by visualizing your inner child in a comfortable environment (I will be using the inner child in this example) and have the following dialogue:

Interviewer—"Are you willing to communicate with me?"

If for any reason you get an answer of no, then ask, "What do you need or want from me in order to feel comfortable enough to express yourself to me?"

Subject—Trust your first thought and answer.

If your inner being is totally unwilling to communicate, then you are either not ready, in that you have not built enough trust, or you should have a friend with you if you are alone. If your inner being ultimately gives you some indication of its willingness to communicate, then proceed.

Interviewer—"What are you feeling?"

Subject—Answer or express the emotion.

Your answer may not come as words such as "I'm feeling sad," but only a sense of the emotion.

Interviewer—"Where are you feeling this in your body?"

Subject—Pause before answering and listen to your body.

Even if the emotion was not given a name, you will still be able to feel a sensation in your body. These sensations may be clear or only vague, but if you scan your body slowly you will find a sensation that seems to stand out, at least slightly. Next, you will focus on the sensations in more detail.

Interviewer—"What does it look like?"

Subject—Accept your first impressions without judgment.
Notice its shape, size, color, texture—rough or smooth, dense and solid or airy and light—what material it is made of—wood, metal, tar, sand paper, etc. Focus on as many details as possible. When you are getting a pretty good sense of this, let the interviewer know, then proceed.

Interviewer—"What sounds are associated with it?"

Subject—Let these sounds out.
They may be moans, groans, scream, vowel sounds, etc.

Interviewer—"What movement goes with this feeling?"

Subject—Let yourself move according to your feelings.
For example, if you are feeling contracted, get into a ball. If more outward expression is called for, then move your arms and legs, perhaps by pounding your feet and arms on the bed or floor. Have pillows under your fists and feet so you don't hurt yourself. Follow your impulses, or simply remain still if that is what you are feeling.

Interviewer—When you sense that they have had enough time to express nonverbally, ask, "What do you want to say that you have not been able to say?"

Subject—If you are sufficiently focused on your emotions and body sensations rather than letting your mind lead the way, some simple but meaningful words will arise. Repeat them a number of times without judging them in any way.

As you focus on your bodily sensations and move according to your impulses, at some point your emotions will begin to intensify. Although your mind will try to pull you away from your feelings, keep focusing on your bodily sensations. If you feel your mind wandering or focusing on some story, bring your awareness back to your feelings—emotional or bodily. At certain points, key thoughts will surface that come from a different place than the usual mental chatter and can be very helpful to the process. They are usually short and to the point and will move you farther into your feelings—such as "Listen to me," "Let me be me," "Don't leave me." Sometimes these key thoughts act as triggers to take you deeper into your feelings, while other times they can be memories, experiences, or awarenesses that help you realize what is blocking you regarding a certain issue.

It is normal for the emotions to come in waves, strong and intense for a while, then less intense. There may be a few waves before you feel complete. When you allow yourself to fully experience the process, giving full attention to your body sensations and expressing movements and sounds, you will naturally evolve into the release phase. Whether it is deep sobbing that attends sadness or grief or a more energized body release that might accompany anger, as the emotion is fully experienced the held energy is simultaneously released.

When you allow yourself to fully feel and express the feelings without resistance or judgment, or on the other side of the spectrum, without pressure or demand for the feelings to arise, you will find that at a point, you will experience a sense of coming out on the other side. These particular feelings will have run their course.

Interviewer—Make sure there are two pillows set up on the floor facing each other, then ask, "Are you ready to have a talk with your inner child?"

Subject—When you feel complete with the release, it is time to have a dialogue between the nurturing parent within you and your inner child (or your higher self and the particular part).

While sitting on one of the two pillows, speak as the nurturing parent. When the child responds, move over to the other pillow and assume the position that you imagine your inner child would take. It is best to verbalize this dialogue out loud. You can strengthen the feeling of being the inner child by holding a pillow or teddy bear during this conversation.

Nurturing parent—Start by acknowledging the inner child for all that it has shared with you, and let it know it is safe. Tell it that things are different now (if you were working with a childhood issue) and that you love it and will be there for it. Trust your intuition about what needs to be said. End by asking the child what it needs to feel supported by you, both now and in daily life.

Move to the child's seat and let the child answer this question.

When the child is finished, move back to the other seat and make a commitment to honor the child's needs to the best of your ability. You can move back and forth until you feel complete. It is best to end by affectionately holding the pillow or teddy bear that represents the inner child.

After this exercise, you will no longer be bound by the deeply held fear of experiencing your emotions because you know you can feel them and still survive. Your inner being expends a lot of energy and comes up with many tactics to help protect you from ever having to experience these emotions. You are now free to make new choices about what you want to believe and create. It is most effective at this point to do some work with your beliefs. (See Chapter 10 for further discussion of beliefs). Once you have fully completed this cycle of working with a deep emotion and the beliefs associated with it, you will have released the limiting hold that this core emotion has had on you. In time other issues will come up for clearing if you stay open and are willing. The results of increased energy, positive changes in your relationships, or enhanced levels of creativity will inspire you to continue on the journey.

chapter
Ten
Uncovering the Beliefs That Shape Your Outer Circumstances

At the core of everything we say and do are our beliefs about ourselves, others, and life. These beliefs come from many sources—from our upbringing, from our experiences and the meanings we give those experiences, from our culture, and from traditions passed down from generation to generation.

Our beliefs affect our reality. Our minds act as filtering systems, canceling out anything that doesn't support our beliefs. For example, if you believe that people are basically good, your mind will keep finding circumstances to support this, even if all around you people are doing bad things. Likewise, if your basic belief is that people cannot be trusted, you will attract people and circumstances that support this belief. Have you ever thought about buying a certain kind of car, and suddenly you see them everywhere? Although cars of that brand have not increased, your heightened awareness makes them more visible. The same thing happens with beliefs.

Beliefs are very powerful. We can decide to change our life and agree to do whatever it takes; establishing new behaviors, saying new things to ourselves, and looking at our experiences differently. Then suddenly we may feel like we run broadside into a wall and land right back where we started. We wonder what went wrong.

The answer usually lies in our beliefs, particularly *core beliefs* that are associated with emotional experiences from the past. Examples are: "I am not enough." "There is not enough." "I am unlovable or unworthy." Tapping into the emotion associated with these beliefs helps us discover and release the buried belief. The emotional release work discussed in Chapter 9, is useful for uncovering these core beliefs. It may be possible to access some core beliefs without tapping the emotion, but something different happens when awareness of the belief surfaces with the emotion.

> *Freeing the energy connected with the emotion simultaneously frees the energy that would otherwise hold the belief in place.*

When this step is missed, just repeating positive statements about what you want—*affirmations*—will usually not be enough to alter the belief's effect. We also hold many beliefs and rules about life that are not associated with emotionally charged experiences, and to discover and release them may not require working with emotions.

At the end of this chapter are a number of exercises for uncovering and working with your beliefs including one focusing on limiting core beliefs. Even without emotional release work you can access some of these simply by *stream of consciousness* writing which is writing quickly, without much thought with a specific question or topic in mind.

When I first did this stream of consciousness exercise concerning core beliefs, this is some of what came up for me:

"I'm not good enough."

"I get love and attention when I am feeling weak, unhappy, untogether." (I received the most nurturing from my mother primarily when I was sick or down.)

"I get love and attention when I am needed for something or good at something." (My mother needed me for emotional support; my dad valued performance and ability).

"Life is tough and stressful."

"There is never enough time, energy, money, or love." (My parents grew up during the Depression when there was never enough. This is a common belief of people of the Depression era and gets passed on.)

The idea is not to blame but to see what hidden beliefs run us so we can make new choices in our lives. If we go through life unaware of the game we are playing and the internal rules of our game, how can we win? The following are examples of some other limiting beliefs:

"Girls aren't smart."

"I can't succeed without a college education."

"Children are (which translates to, I am) better seen than heard."

"My race is inferior."

"Others suffer or lose when I win or get what I want."

"Expressing myself causes pain to me or others."

"What I have to say is unimportant."

"I am unimportant."

"Others are more important than I am."

It is interesting that sometimes we live out such beliefs, while other times we go to the extreme opposite, rebelling against what we saw or heard. For example, the belief "what I have to say is unimportant" may make someone always want to be heard. This person may act as if they know everything and not do much listening.

Another way to discover your limiting beliefs is to access what your primary caretakers or important authority figures told you or led you to believe. In addition, you can listen to your self talk when you make a positive belief statement. (See the awareness exercises in the Try It section.)

We can also deduce from our experience what beliefs we may be holding. If something isn't working for us, we can ask ourselves: "What belief must I have about myself or life in order to be experiencing this?" For example, if you find that every time you seem to amass some money it just disappears, and you were given a strong message that there is not enough of anything to go around, you may deduce that you have a belief that "the more I have, the less there is for others." Your guilt about having money can keep you from ever really having it. Or you could believe that you are not worthy, money is evil, or success is bad.

Beliefs can be categorized as:

- *Personal*, as in "I am" or "I am not,"
- *Global*, as in "people are" or "life is,"
- *Rules*, as in "if, then." (For example, if you work hard then you will succeed. Most of us weren't told if you love what you do then you'll succeed.)

Whatever form our beliefs take, the effect is the same: our beliefs determine what happens to us.

After you have examined your core beliefs, it is helpful to look at your rules and general beliefs as they relate to specific areas that you may not have touched on. For example, look at your beliefs about work, money, relationships, people, life, effort and reward, time, men, women, and so forth. Keep the beliefs that serve you, then select new beliefs regarding areas of your life that don't work.

One of the first steps to changing anything is awareness. Once you are aware of what beliefs are controlling you, you can then make new choices. Becoming aware of the limiting beliefs we hold is an important step in freeing ourselves to be more of who we truly are.

After acquiring a full inventory of beliefs that are getting in your way, whether by an emotional healing, writing process, or noticing what isn't working in life and deducing what belief that must involve, it is time for some form of release ritual prior to adopting new beliefs. The unconscious *speaks to us* and tells us things about ourselves through the emotions, intuition, stream of consciousness writing, metaphors, and dreams. We *talk to* the unconscious through ritual. We can tell it what we want to let go of or what new things we want to take on. Ritual has been used through the centuries as a healthful means of transition and transformation.

For example, you can create a burning bowl ceremony for the list of limiting beliefs. This can be as simple as lighting a match to the paper and saying emphatically, "I now release these limiting beliefs." Or it can be done more elaborately with an alter and prayers, or in nature at a campfire. What matters most is your degree of intention. The more energy you put into the ceremony, the more effective will be your statement to your unconscious and Spirit.

In one ceremony for myself, I made an alter of beautiful items that had meaning to me. Then I put a special chair in front of it and draped a beautiful cloth over the chair, putting other objects of beauty or meaning around the chair. Next, I lit candles on the alter, then meditated and prayed to be released from my limiting beliefs and shown anything else I needed. After this I burned the paper in a ceramic bowl and sang a chant, which consisted of sounds I let out as the spirit moved me. Then, shaking a rattle, I walked around the chair and the objects, which were set up with a key one in each direction—north, south, east, and west—and said affirmations and prayed for what I wanted for myself, others, and the earth. Finally, standing in the middle, I let out a few more sounds and sang a song of gratitude.

How elaborate you want to get is entirely up to you. There are no rules for such ceremonies, other than to be true to yourself and do what feels good to you, though stretching out of your comfort zone a little is helpful. If rituals of this nature are not appealing, you might try to incorporate a "throwing off" type body movement with your statements.

More possibilities for release are described at the end of this chapter.

After you have released the limiting beliefs with a ritual, it is time to create new empowering beliefs. Write affirmative statements that are the opposite of each limiting belief. For example, some of the affirmative statements to my core limiting beliefs were:

"I am more than good enough just as I am. I am worthy of abundant love, success, health, and joy."

"I am lovable just as I am, even when I am strong, powerful, happy and successful."

"I am lovable just as I am, without having to do, be, or give anything."

"Life is fun and easy for me."

"There is more than enough of everything: time, energy, money, and love."

These statements specifically counteracted the particular core beliefs that I had held. On a daily basis I would read the limiting beliefs list and start out by saying, "I now release these old limiting beliefs." When I read the new list I would say, "I now adopt and absorb these new empowering beliefs." Eventually I dropped the limiting beliefs list and just read the empowering list. It is very effective to read the new beliefs out loud, even looking in the mirror as you say them or adding movement.

Visualization is another way to reprogram yourself with your new, more desired beliefs. Visualization is holding in your mind's eye the image of what you want to do, be or feel. In a study done with basketball players, a group practiced foul-line shots and another group practiced through detailed visualization only. When tested later, both groups got essentially equal scores. Visualization can be strengthened by adding emotion (described in the Try It section).

In Chapter 2, I listed six steps for personal change. Working with our beliefs can follow these steps. First, we set an intention to become aware of what is controlling us or causing results we are not happy with (*willingness*). Then we become aware of what we are doing that doesn't work and the associated beliefs we are holding (*awareness*). We can then feel the associated feelings (*being with*), release the stored energy (*release*), and input the new beliefs we would rather hold (*transformation*). The last, essential step is to put the new way into practice (*changing behavior*). Every time you see yourself acting according to the old beliefs, notice what you are doing or about to do; then consciously choose a new behavior based on your new beliefs. The exercises in the Try It section are grouped according to these steps.

TRY IT!

There are a number of steps for transforming limiting beliefs. Though it is possible to go through them all in a short period, it is helpful to take your time. Try working with the key issue that is presenting itself in your life at the moment. Having strong feelings about wanting something to change greatly enhances the effectiveness of the process. Notice what isn't working in your life right now or has upset you. Then focus on that area of life.

1 | Willingness

Ask yourself this question, "Am I fully willing to know what has been holding me back, to face whatever I find, and to do whatever it takes to make the necessary changes?" If you can say yes to this then you are opening a door that will help the truths to be revealed.

2 | Accessing Awareness of Limiting Beliefs

All of these exercises can be enhanced by deep breathing and moving to rhythmic music before sitting down to write. Movement and breathing combined with stream of consciousness writing will help you access your subconscious.

❑ Make a separate list for each of the following that applies to you: "What my father, mother, primary childhood caretaker, or significant childhood figure taught me to believe" (through words, actions, or implications). Quickly write everything that comes to mind—both empowering and limiting.

❑ Write at the top of a piece of paper: "Limiting Core Beliefs." Go within and ask yourself, "What are the bottom line beliefs that are limiting me the most?" Write your answers. On another paper write "Empowering Core Beliefs," and ask yourself, "What are the beliefs that support me most?" Write your answers.

Another way to do this exercise is to write all of your beliefs at once, without attempting to separate them into the two categories of limiting and empowering. This way you don't inhibit your stream of thought and won't start denigrating yourself for being so "untogether" when you only see the limiting beliefs. You can separate them into two categories when you are finished.

❑ Complete the following sentences:
  ❑ I am most afraid people will find out ___.
  ❑ I can't make it in life (or succeed in a particular area) because I am ___.
  ❑ The reason I can't have what I want is because ___.
  ❑ What I am most afraid is true about me is ___.
  ❑ My most negative thought about me is ___.

❑ Write a specific affirmation (positive statement about yourself or life) on the left side of the page. On the right side, write everything that pops into your head as you write the affirmation. After this, write the affirmation again on the left side and repeat the process. Rewrite the affirmation and your internal response until you have at least ten responses. For example, on the left might be: "I am now doing work I love and am making good money for it." What might surface in relationship to this are thoughts such as the following: "Yeah, fat chance, I have no training, I'm not smart enough." Or, you might make the statement: "I am feeling peaceful and relaxed and have plenty of time to do everything that I need and want to do." And you might get the response: "There's way too much to do, that's impossible, only the rich have enough money to be relaxed." If you do this with the intention of finding out what you really feel, all kinds of things will surface.

The next two exercises will help flush out many hidden beliefs relating to specific areas of your life that have not yet surfaced in the previous exercises. Once you become aware of the beliefs that can be sabotaging your best efforts to move forward you can then use any of them in the exercises that follow.

❑ Make a list of your rules and beliefs, both limiting and empowering, for specific areas of your life that you would like to work on. Possibilities include money, relationships, career or service contribution, health or body, life in general, authority, men, women, and so forth. Do this by writing the subject on the top of the page and recording every belief you have about it that comes to mind, both positive and negative. When you are finished, choose which beliefs seem to have the strongest effect in counteracting what it is you want for yourself, then work on transforming those.

❑ Look at each complaint or area of dissatisfaction in your life and write down the answer to this question: "What belief must I have about myself or life in order to be experiencing this?"

3 | Being With

❑ From any or all of the previous exercises, create one list of all the beliefs and rules that are holding you back. Take time to read and really be with the effects of holding these beliefs so long. Close your eyes, breathe, and experience the harsh reality of what you could have done or been if you had not been holding these beliefs. Next, imagine how your life will progress if you continue to hold these beliefs for years to come—for one year, five, ten, or even twenty. What will the repercussions be on not only your life but your family or children's lives? Let yourself completely be with the feelings that surface. I recommend focusing on the repercussion of the limiting beliefs because people are often more motivated by moving away from pain than moving toward pleasure. Consequently letting yourself feel the pain of the lost potential from holding these beliefs will often provide strong motivation for moving forward.

❑ Being with feelings and emotions as described in Chapter 9 can greatly assist the process of bringing beliefs to the surface and diminishing their emotional hold.

4 | Releasing

Now that you have accessed many of your limiting beliefs and felt what the cost has been and might be for holding them, you are ready to begin the work of letting go and transforming these beliefs and the deeply rooted behavior patterns connected with them.

❑ Burning bowl ceremony—simple or elaborate (see page 132 in this chapter for details.)

❑ Body movement: Taking each of the limiting beliefs, say emphatically, "I now release ___." With each statement, make a release movement, such as quickly and firmly throwing out your arms or kicking your legs. Or bend over with your head upside down and shake your arms, head, and chest while making your statement. Or run your hands over your arms and legs in a brushing-off motion. Adding sounds or deep breathing will empower this process even more.

❑ A more peaceful release technique for limiting beliefs is to incorporate a release affirmation while doing yoga or stretching. While holding a stretch position, either silently or out loud say, "I now release ___."

❑ Another process that works well for many people is one adapted from Leonard Laskow's book *Healing With Love*[10]. Take a deep breath in while you think of the belief, hold the breath a few seconds, then let the air out forcefully as you say, "I release ___ (the belief)." Do this for each belief separately, repeating it a few times.

❑ If you want to keep the release process really simple, just read your list out loud. Start by saying, "I now release these limiting beliefs." Whether you do a release ritual or not, it is a good idea to read your release list each day along with your new list (see the first section under Transformation below), until it no longer feels necessary.

5 | Transformation

❑ For each of the limiting beliefs accessed, write an affirmative statement that is the positive opposite of each limiting belief. (See examples of this on page 133 of this chapter.)

❑ Make a commitment to yourself to read your new list of empowering beliefs every day for one week. You can enhance the reading by standing in front of a mirror, making eye contact with yourself and stating your new empowering beliefs. If you like the resulting feeling, renew this commitment a week at a time.

❑ You can also empower your statements by incorporating body movements of receiving with each positive affirmation, preferably outdoors. Separate your feet, point your knees over your toes, then bend your knees and make a large swooping action with your arms, first reaching down to the earth and then up to the heavens, and finally moving your arms to your center. Or just reach up to the heavens with your arms in a raised and open position ready to receive while you make the statements. Add a deep inhalation to breathe the affirming statement into your being. Bringing the body into the process and using the voice helps anchor the statement into your subconscious.

❑ Another possibility is to incorporate these new belief statements with yoga. If you made stretching movements with release statements, now use more active postures that require some holding and strength while repeating the affirmation statements.

❑ Pick one of the new beliefs and visualize a desired result that could occur from having this new belief. For example, if the new belief is "I deserve to be loved," the result would be a loving relationship. See yourself and another loving person engaged in a particular activity in as much detail as possible, including the sights, sounds, and smells of the environment and the physical sensations such as a touch on the cheek or the wind against the face.

Add emotion to enhance the effect of the visualization. To do this, put the first image aside for a few moments and remember a time you experienced the desired emotion that goes along with this picture. For example, remember a time when you felt truly loved. Perhaps it was during your childhood or at the beginning of a relationship. If you never have had the desired experience, imagine how you believe it would feel. As you recall this experience in as much detail as possible, allow the feelings associated with it to emerge. Then in your mind replace the old image with the new visualization. Connecting this mental process with the emotions felt from an earlier experience will more deeply root the new belief and help create the desired result.

6 | Behavior Change

Watch your words and actions in daily life, noticing whether they come from your old beliefs or your new ones. If they come from your old beliefs and attitudes, practice new behaviors that reflect the new belief. Don't judge yourself, simply observe and practice. (More on this in Chapter 14.)

Reclaiming Your Soul—
eleven
The Shamanic Tradition

A book such as this covering all aspects of self-healing and growth would be incomplete without discussing shamanic practices. Many ancient indigenous cultures have much to offer our modern-day life. For instance, incorporating song, dance, and rhythm into our busy lives, particularly when experienced as part of community, can be an invaluable practice for health and happiness. These indigenous cultures also offer valuable healing methods for working with psychospiritual issues.

The line is very thin between shamanism and some of the current healing modalities. The shamanic concept of "soul loss," seen as a root cause of many psychological or physical problems, is congruent with contemporary views of psychoimmunoneurology, a medical term used for the body-mind connection. There are similarities between shamanism and psychology—use of altered states of consciousness (ASC), a prime example. Charles Tart, who does research on states of consciousness describes an ASC as a "qualitative alteration in the overall pattern of mental function, such that the experiencer feels consciousness is radically different from the way it functions ordinarily."[11] Tart compares an ASC to computer functioning—when we change the input we get a different output.

Psychotherapist Jeannette Gagan, in her book *Journeying* shows how psychology and shamanism both incorporate ASCs. Referring to that part of the unconscious mind that "is the receptacle for healing forces," she states that in an ASC the thought processes may be changed and the boundary between the conscious and the unconscious becomes more fluid. A fluid relationship between the conscious and unconscious is central to psychological health.[12] Gagan reminds us that when we move into an altered state carrying the intention for healing, the potential exists for tapping into a realm of healing resources.

In shamanism an ASC, also called "*nonordinary reality*," is brought about through ritual—which can include invocation, a steady drum beat, chanting, dancing, changes in lighting, music, or the arrangement of power objects. In psychological practices an ASC is induced through concentrated focus on subtle body sensations, emotionally charged conversation, deep breathing, hypnotic induction, guided imagery, or biofeedback.

Both schools of thought, shamanism and psychology, also incorporate imagery. A psychologist will use visualization, guided imagery, and voice dialogue with different imagined parts of the client. A shaman will "journey"—travel to the *lower world, middle world*, or *upper world*. Each of these worlds contains distinct images and information to be brought back. The lower world is comprised of natural landscapes such as jungles, forests, mountains, deserts, or bodies of water. Here the journeyor interacts with the spirits of such inhabitants as the fish, insects, or animals. Any one of these "spirit beings" can step forward to become the person's "power animal" and personal guide or ally, both on the journey and throughout life. The power animal will transmit certain characteristics and strengths as well as give guidance and direction when summoned to do so. The middle world resembles the world we live in, but traverses barriers of time. A shaman will travel to this realm in order to retrieve a lost part of your soul if the shaman determines that "soul loss" is the problem. The upper world, usually somewhere above the clouds, is the world of elevated or divine beings, any one of whom can step forward to be your personal guide, teacher, or benefactor. In addition, as Gagan points out: "Imagery has been central to the work of indigenous shamans. The shaman today, like his ancestors, is able to 'see' an invasion of foreign energy encased in his patient's body, 'hear' the call of a lost soul, and 'feel' the brush of his power animal against his leg."[12]

> *Whether the journey takes place in another dimension of reality, as claimed by shamans, or in the imagination, as held by psychologists, it crosses a barrier between the conscious and unconscious and often leads to healing.*

In many shamanic traditions, psychological as well as physical problems are often attributed to *soul loss*. This soul loss is usually caused by trauma. You could say part of the soul becomes lost in another dimension of time and space. The traumatic event might be obviously devastating, such as physical abuse, or seemingly mundane, such as watching your mother smash your just built model airplane because you didn't come when called, or not being picked for a team you had your heart set on. Soul loss can also occur from repeated degradation or the ongoing emotional unavailability of someone you love very much.

Two common healing practices in shamanism are *soul retrieval*, in which the shaman travels to find and return the lost part of your soul, and *extraction*, in which the shaman "sees" foreign energy in your body, such as may occur if someone is extremely spiteful toward you, and removes it.

Soul retrieval is a powerful life-changing event, and although it is best undertaken by a shamanic practitioner, I believe that a practitioner may not always be necessary. Just as you can learn to journey on your own to contact your power animals, you can learn to conduct a soul retrieval for yourself.

I first experienced a soul retrieval when I was at an important crossroads in my life. Having followed the path of growth outlined in this book for some time, I had decided to open up another period of time for focusing attention on some deeply ingrained, nonproductive patterns in my life. What began to emerge was a discernible sensation in my chest that felt like a heavy weight sitting over my heart. At one point I described it as having a shroud over my chest and another time as a ball the size of a pea but with a density that made it heavier than any known element. At the same time, I was facing the issue of what was my right work. It seemed that no matter what work I had done over the years, something felt "wrong" with all of it, even though I had been helping people and had been successful by most standards. At this point I had been leading powerful week-long personal growth retreats using many of the processes presented in this book. As wonderful as this was, still there was a part of me that didn't feel all there.

I considered many possibilities for the source of my feeling of dissatisfaction. Having such strong feelings of dissatisfaction with my work, especially when I was making such a difference in people's lives, didn't make sense to me. I had worked through a lot on my insecurity and lack of self-confidence as a leader and teacher. From the perspective of my inner child I had made great strides with these issues. At that time I did not make any correlation between the heavy feeling in my chest and the issue of dissatisfaction in my work.

Around this same time, the strength of my intention to understand what was happening caused some deep feelings to surface. As I allowed myself to fully experience what was coming up, without reverting to my usual avoidance tactic of too much to do, I began to sink into a deep place of lethargy. I lost all motivation and faith in everything I believed in and had been teaching for so long, even though I had seen these teachings bring about major transformations for many people. The only thing that still brought me comfort and joy was being in nature.

One day while I was sitting at one of my favorite spots on some lovely warm flat rocks by a natural pool with a small waterfall, I allowed myself to surrender into this place of no motivation even more deeply than I had done before. As a result, I came to a place of accepting that I might never make a difference. To me, worse than any of the other consequences of lacking motivation was that I wouldn't make a difference in this world. I could see how attached I had been to "making a difference." I experienced an important passage when I was able to accept myself as a valuable human being worthy of Spirit's love—even if I never made a difference.

Later that day a woman appeared who would play a significant role in steering me toward my soul retrieval. Without my saying anything, this woman, who had great psychic and intuitive abilities, described what I had been feeling, telling me it was like a net across my chest (I had called it a shroud). She said it had something to do with a past life and that I was greatly holding back my power as a leader and healer because of it. She also told me that I was to do a vision quest.

Shortly after that I visited a friend who is a highly respected hypnotherapist. When he mentioned a story involving a past life regression he had done for someone, I immediately asked if he would do one for me. Before this, I didn't see any value in past life regression because I thought, "if you don't know whether it's true, what good is it?" For whatever reason, it felt right to try one at that time. When he put me in a hypnotic state, I was careful not to make up things, I simply let images arise in my mind. What came out of that session was an amazing story that perfectly explained why I had felt resistant to being a practitioner or facilitator of the different healing modalities I had been involved with over the last eighteen years and at the same time so compelled to do them. As a result, many pieces of my life and work story began to make sense. Without going into all the details of the story, what I got was, the healer or shaman in me had given up the medicine and was left feeling disheartened.

A healing occurred with that experience and more was still to come. With the new awareness about this aspect of my soul and without my knowing exactly what I was doing, I performed a soul retrieval that caused a dramatic shift in my whole being. In response to the psychic woman's urging, I immediately made plans to go on a vision quest. While on the vision quest, I created a *medicine wheel*—a large circle of stones on the ground with a larger stone at each of the four directions, along with something symbolic for each element—fire, water, earth, and air. I spent considerable time walking in a clockwise circle around the wheel and praying. During the past life regression, when asked a question about what the person from an earlier time was feeling, I clearly answered, "Disheartened." Just before the trip I had read in Angeles Arrien's book *Four Fold Way*, that disheartenment is associated with soul loss. This made an impression on me, so I started to pray and call out to my soul, beseeching it to rejoin me and reassuring it that things were different now. At the time, I didn't know what I was doing and simply did what felt right.

Not long after the trip, my energy picked up and I began saying things to people like, "I feel part of life again, I want to participate in life now." I started to feel motivated and enthusiastic. A few months later I was drawn to a book, Sandra Ingerman's *Soul Retrieval*, that explained to me what had happened. She told many stories of people for whom she performed soul retrievals. Before their soul retrievals they had also said they felt lifeless and lacked motivation and, like me, afterwards felt part of life once again.

A shamanic healer will go in search of your lost soul, locate the place, experience, and aspect of your soul that is gone, then "blow it" back to you. While it is best to have a shamanic practitioner per-form this, it may not always be possible to find an appropriate indi-vidual. I believe that you can have a similar experience by taking the following steps.

The first step is to uncover the experiences that resulted in your soul being "frozen in time." Some shamanic practitioners don't be-lieve in past lives; whether you believe in past lives or not, I recom-mend starting with your current life because there are often many parts of your soul to work with in this life alone. As I mentioned in Chapter 2 the process starts with your willingness, which will evolve into awareness. Though awareness can come from your own inter-nal journey, it helps to have support from a counselor, hypnotherapist, or other professional, which often speeds up the process. It is also important to let yourself feel what this lost part of your soul felt, whether through a full emotional release or simply through naming the emotion—just as I was able to say I felt dis-heartened. I believe my willingness to be with my feelings of heavi-ness and loss of motivation is what attracted the rest of the healing process to me, bringing that woman to me on the rocks and all the other serendipitous events that occurred after that.

Once you know more about what aspect of your soul is lost, including the circumstances under which your soul "checked out," you are ready to "retrieve" your soul. This process involves shaking a rattle or having someone beat a drum at a slow steady pace. This creates a natural trance state that helps to shift the part of the brain you are operating from. Then, through strong intention, which may take the form of prayer to a higher power for help, and entreatment to that lost part of your soul, you can usually retrieve it. Sometimes it takes more coaxing, for example, talking to that part, letting it know that 1) you respect its choice, 2) things are different now, and it is safe to return, 3) you are here to help, and 4) not only is it unnecessary to stay where it is, but things will be a lot better and more fun if it will come back to you.

According to shamanism, not only is soul loss a source of distress, it can also be due to "*possession*." This takes the form of an energetic holding pattern that can pervade an aspect of the inner being or a physical organ or can encompass the whole be-ing. The concept is that a being holds your soul captive due to such feelings as jealousy, vengeance, a broken heart, or fear. I believe this energy form can also be created by our own thoughts or passed through the genes from generation to generation. The following is a story of a powerful shamanic healing I experienced which released the hold a very persistent energy had on me.

After experiencing a number of relationship disappointments, I realized I was still holding a deeply rooted belief that said: "I am not enough, I am not fully lovable as I am." I had already done considerable emotional work related to this issue, so I began to say many affirmations to counterbalance this feeling. But because there was still a blockage that was incongruent to what I was saying, these affirmations began to stir up something in me. I would go to bed each night and wake up each morning with a heavy feeling in my chest. It was a different sensation than the one I had had in my chest related to never being satisfied with my work. As I let myself be with this feeling, I came to recognize its deep roots of loneliness and sadness. I also felt another layer of anxiety, a fear for my survival, as if I might become so poor that I would starve and die. I knew this was irrational since in my everyday life I was experiencing abundance and felt love and appreciation from many people. But such deeply rooted beliefs and issues are often not logical.

After about two months of religiously saying counterbalancing affirmations, I woke up with a complete understanding of what was going on. This limiting program and the feelings associated with it were not actually mine. (I had done much clearing and healing work of what had come from my own life, and in addition, the nature of my childhood did not warrant the intensity of what I was feeling.) It became clear that though I was experiencing the weight in my own body, it was due to my matriarchal lineage rather than my own experience. My mother had had a very hard and lonely life; her father had left when she was two, her mother had died when she was ten, and she had suffered abject poverty as well as a succession of rejections and losses. I realized that an energetic, cellular thought form had been handed down through my genes and was stuck to me like glue, despite all the work I had done. In that moment, I knew that it was time to use some form of cellular reprogramming and energy work to lift this pattern from me.

I believe up leveling our lives is an eclectic process. Sometimes the work may be connected with the physical body; other times it may be more concerned with the mental body, the emotional body, or the energetic body. At this point in my journey it was time for some energetic healing work. I believe that much shamanic work deals with the energetic body. In her book *Soul Retrieval*, Sandra Ingerman tells many stories of individuals who did not get much out of their therapy until other energetic issues, such as those associated with soul retrieval, were dealt with. When they went back to therapy, they made great progress. It is often necessary to work with the whole being rather than only with one aspect.

On the day I woke with the awareness of this maternal energetic pattern, I went to church, where one of the participants introduced an American Indian shaman who was visiting her. I asked if he would work with me, and later that day I was blessed with a session where he did an *extraction*. By this time I had studied quite a bit about indigenous healers and recognized by his technique that he was what is called a "sucking doctor." With a hot coal between his teeth, he sucked the energetic form out of my heart area and spit a black slimy substance into a bowl. When he was finished, I could feel that something had lifted and after this I never experienced the heavy feeling in my chest again. A very clear energetic shift had occurred, and after a few months, my life circumstances began to reflect this shift in many wonderful ways, including the manifestation of a powerful and lasting relationship.

I believe we can combine the two approaches of modern-day psychospiritual healing with more ancient shamanic practices. It is often a combination of all the many aspects of self-transformation that allows us to change old patterns and lead more creative and fulfilling lives.

TRY IT!

1 | Finding Your Power Animal

Traveling to find your power animal is called *journeying*. Begin in a manner similar to that described in the Critical Incident Exercise, with deep relaxation and if possible with shamanic drumming, either live or recorded. You will be descending into the lower world, which is described in this chapter.

To enter this world, allow an image to arise that contains an opening into the earth, such as an animal's hole in the ground, a tree trunk with a large opening, under or behind a waterfall, a whirlpool in a body of water, or a cave. See yourself stepping into one of these portals of descent, then allow yourself to sink down.

Keep descending until the image of a natural landscape comes up before you, such as a rock canyon, forest, jungle, ocean bottom, stream, or cavern. Become aware of as many details as possible, not only what you see, but also the sounds, smells, and textures. Notice what creatures come up to you. One school of thought states that if the creature—animal, bird, fish or even some insects—approaches you three times, then it is your power animal. It is also suggested that you ask it if it is your power animal. If it says yes, then spend some time with it. You can ask its name, but this is for you alone, not to be shared. Follow it and see where it takes you. It may offer you a ride on its back.

This first journey may be just to meet it or, as in the case of subsequent journeys, you may have a question or problem in mind before you begin. Your power animal may give you insight by speaking to you in words, by demonstration, by metaphor, or by imparting its qualities to you. Before returning, ask what you can do for it.

When you feel complete, go back up the way you came. If someone is drumming for you, a faster drum beat signifies time to return.

Immediately write down what you experienced and the insight you gained from the power animal. Ask yourself what aspects and qualities this animal possesses and how you can bring these into your life. Once you find your power animals they become your allies whom you can turn to anytime.

2 | Critical Incident Process

The following is a hypnotherapy exercise created by Dr. Irv Katz.[13] It is used to access key points in your life where critical decisions were made that effect you for years to come and for ascertaining points of soul loss. If you are interested in past life work it can also be used to explore past lives. If you relax and trust your intuition and higher self, this exercise can show you where you are stuck and help you uncover any "soul loss." It is best to do this work with a professional, either a therapist versed in this type of work or a shamanic practitioner. However if this is not possible, you can work through this process yourself or find a friend you trust and have them work with you. They can walk you through each step as you report to them what you are experiencing. If you do it alone read it through a few times first then get comfortable, close your eyes, and walk yourself through the steps. Don't rush or be impatient; Allow images, thoughts, words, or feelings to surface.

❑ Choose a problem, something you would like to see changed in your life. Note how this issue limits you and what the benefits will be when transformation takes place. This process is particularly effective for issues that control you or things that resist change despite your best efforts.

❑ Get very relaxed. If someone is helping you, have them walk you through your body parts, suggesting you deeply relax each part. Suggestive words like relax, ease, melt, and sink will be helpful. You could also approach this in a shamanic style by having someone beat a steady, repetitive rhythm on a drum or play a recording of shamanic trance drumming. Listening to very peaceful music is also good, as is silence. If you are alone, imagine each part of your body deeply relaxing until it feels very still, almost weightless, and your mind begins to slow down. Focus your attention on the rhythm of your breath.

❑ When in this relaxed state, imagine you are in a building tall enough that the floor you are on coincides with your age. If you choose to use this as a past life regression, start in the present, and let the floors represent eras in history.

❑ Imagine you are stepping into an elevator. When the button is pressed, the doors will close to the present time.

❑ Go down the elevator of time. Your unconscious will direct your hand to the appropriate button, which will take you to a time and place that is connected to a circumstance and a consequent decision that gave rise to the present pattern—"the critical incident." (A shamanic practitioner doing a soul retrieval finds this for you. In this process you will find it.) It is fine if you have no conscious idea, just let your intuition and higher self guide you, trusting the process. You can see the numbers for each floor light up or just feel yourself going farther and farther down until the elevator arrives at some lower floor. The incident that you come upon may turn out to be dramatic or seem rather innocuous. It could simply be an experience that "broke the camel's back" after cumulative prior experiences, causing a dramatic shift to occur.

❑ When the elevator stops and the doors open, step through them into a hallway with many doors.

❑ The door you need to open is labeled "circumstance and issue to be resolved."
Note: It is not unusual for there to be some resistance to experiencing what is behind the door. You can employ cre-

ative strategies to help with this such as:

- ❑ If you are too small to reach the doorknob, stand on a stool.
- ❑ If the door is locked, have someone bring a key.
- ❑ If the door is stuck, have two hefty body guards help open it.
- ❑ If you are too frightened to open the door, peek through the keyhole.
- ❑ If it is too dark, have a candle or flashlight appear or assume the power to see in the dark.

❑ When you open the door, you will experience the incident or circumstance. If it is too traumatic, you can just observe what is happening. Describe this out loud to your helper.

❑ Ask yourself, "What decisions did I make at this time about life, people, and how I should be or act?" It is probable that the decision made sense for that particular age and situation.

❑ Using the image of a VCR tape that is scrolling, review your life from the time behind the door forward to the present. From the perspective of your higher self, notice how the decision has affected your life and especially how it has limited and is still limiting your life.

❑ Now begin to rewrite history with the intent of emotional release and enacting a new encoding process. Say what you would have liked to say then but did not, and experience what you did not let yourself feel. Any helper present may act as a surrogate, playing the role of ideal parent, loving relative, accepting figure, and so forth. If no one is assisting you, call up an aspect of yourself to play the nurturing or wise parent.

❑ Holding a pillow representing your inner child, past life figure, or whatever person or ego state was referred to in the critical incident, allow yourself to come from your most loving, enlightened place and send love and kind words to help heal the wound. Let this person or aspect of yourself know that now they have you to love and protect them, they are not guilty, they did the best they could under the circumstances, and there is no longer a need to defend oneself or maintain the old pattern.

❑ Now you can go back to the elevator with the wound healing and sense that you are your own validating source—your own parent, healer, or therapist. As you pass the floors on your way up, forgive yourself for every time (each age you pass) you protected yourself with the old pattern, understanding that while it is not necessary now, it served a purpose that had a positive intent. If you wish, you can stop at a specific floor on the way back up or even choose to go farther down to focus on another problematic experience.

❑ After you have returned to the present time, hold the pillow again and come from your higher self. Communicate to yourself in a way that reinforces your experience. In this communication, utilize the wisdom available to you now that will support you in realizing a new way of being that truly serves you.

❑ Verbalize out loud your new decision or declaration.

❑ Allow a symbol that reflects your new way of being to surface in your mind, using it as an anchor to reinforce your new attitude and future behaviors. You might want to draw this symbol and put it on a wall as a reminder of your new way of being.

I believe that when you communicate with the part of you that has been injured in the manner described in this process, the effect is similar to someone else going to the lost aspect of soul and retrieving it, as practiced in soul retrieval. If the situation is very difficult, further action could be required. If this is the case, your own ritual calling the lost aspect of soul back can solidify the process. This is what happened for me when I created and walked around the medicine wheel praying for the lost aspect of my soul to return. After this, things began to shift dramatically in regard to the pertinent issue, though it was the process of experiencing the critical incident that opened me up to what had been lost.

twelve

More Tools for the Journey

There are many tools to help us achieve greater mastery of life, some that work with our minds, some that work with our bodies, and others that work with our emotions. Although I have already discussed many tools, I would like to provide a few more for working with the mind that affect our outlook.

The Quality of Your Questions

The use of questions is an effective tool for enhancing life expression. Since I first began to work with questions, it has consistently been one of the most powerful and easy daily tools. The premise of the use of questions is this: much of our "self talk" is in the form of questions, and thus we can redirect our thinking and focus by improving the questions we ask ourselves. Notice how often you've asked yourself such questions as, "Why does this always happen to me?" "Why is life so difficult?" "Why do I always have so many bills and barely enough money to pay them?" "Why do people act like that?" Notice that after the "why" you make a statement—one that reinforces or affirms the very thing you don't want. Even if you don't say it to yourself in exact question form the negative question may still be implied.

Whenever you notice yourself asking a disempowering question, stop and think of a new question that would elicit an answer you would rather experience. For example, if you were to ask, "Why do these things always happen to me?" you could instead ask, "What can I learn from this?" In a situation where you are trying to do things differently but have not made as much progress as you might like, instead of asking, "Why do I always blow it?" you can ask, "How can I be patient with myself until I get it?" or "How can I make it better?"

You can also use this approach to turn a disempowering statement around. For instance, I used to say, "There is not enough time." Now I ask, "What can I do to relax, enjoy the process, and still accomplish my goal?" Or, "How can I be peacefully productive?" This process of turning a disempowering question or statement into a productive question works because you end up affirming a positive statement. When you say, "How can I make this better?" your subconscious picks up, "I can make this better." If you say, "What can I say to turn this situation around?" it picks up, "I can turn this situation around." The subconscious tends to understand everything in the affirmative. That's why, if you are writing affirmations, you should avoid putting a negation in the statement because your mind drops the negation and you end up affirming the very thing you don't want. For instance, the mind hears "I no longer eat sweets" as "I eat sweets." It would be better to say, "I choose to eat only healthful foods." When we make positive statements or ask positive questions, our mind, acting as a filter, focuses on those things that support the statements.

If you don't like the way someone is behaving, or if you don't like the direction an interaction is taking, instead of complaining or getting defensive, which only escalates matters, ask yourself, "What can I do or say that will make this situation better?" I first discovered how powerful this can be when I was talking to a former employee who was also a personal friend. We were talking about a money issue, and the emotional heat started to rise. I wanted to keep my friendship with her, so out of the desperation of the moment, I said a little prayer inside my head. I asked, "What can I say or do that will turn this around so we can both feel satisfied?" Within a few moments, we began to work something out that was mutually agreeable. Now I use this question whenever necessary.

Another way to work with questions is what I call the *affirmative question*. To do this, take any affirmation and turn it into a question. For example, the statement, "I have an energetic healthy body" can be turned into a question, such as, "What must I do in order to have a healthy body?" This not only makes the affirmative statement but also expresses your willingness to do your part to get there. I eventually gave all my affirmation lists a header that read either: "How can I ___," or "What must I see, feel, or do in order to ___." I find the results of working with these questions miraculous, and I get a faster response from them than when I use typical affirmations.

After you state or think your affirmative question, *hold the question* until the answer arises. To hold the question, periodically ask yourself the question without thinking of an answer, waiting for the answer to surface on its own. Sometimes the answer comes quickly, other times it takes time. If you keep asking the question, eventually you will get the answer. Sometimes it seems to just pop out of your mouth, while other times it comes as a sudden hunch or flash of intuition in the back of your mind. Sometimes life circumstances will naturally present the answer. If you want the same old answers, keep asking the same old questions. The well known author and lecturer Tony Robbins says, "If you want the quality of your life to change, change the quality of your questions!"[14]

Reframing

Two doctors, Suzanne Kabasa and Blair Justice, have studied and written about individuals with what they call "psychological hardiness," who, among other positive traits, exhibit strong immune systems. They say there are three characteristics to this hearty personality called the three C's:

- •*Commitment*—Having a sense of meaning and purpose to one's life, usually a commitment to a higher goal or a spiritual belief and faith.

- •*Control*—Believing you have the ability to make choices and the tendency to take responsibility for yourself rather than lay blame on others or see yourself as a helpless victim.

- •*Challenge*—Being able to see changes and other stressful situations as challenges and opportunities for growth, rather than become negative or fearful or give up.

We have already discussed the first two traits; the third trait, challenge, is a perfect example of reframing.

Challenge refers to the ability to take life's punches, seeing them as opportunities for growth, improvement of circumstances, or a chance to become a wiser individual through the experience. Individuals with this perspective believe that everything happens for a higher purpose and that no matter what setbacks occur, they are always moving toward higher ground.

Generally speaking, if you are able to look at life's challenges in this way, you are able to *reframe*. This means you put a new frame around an old picture: you take a given situation (the picture) and give it a new meaning (the frame). Have you ever wondered how two children in the same family may experience the same traumatic events, perhaps one of abuse or emotional abandonment, and one is miserable in life, while the other goes on to success in the world? This is due to the underlying meaning each one gave the experience. "Nothing has any meaning except the meaning we give it."[15]

For example, Carol was raised in a family with an alcoholic mother and a father who left when she was two. She created a set of beliefs that interpreted this kind of experience as meaning she was worthless. From that point on, everything that occurred supported her underrated value of herself and further perpetuated her already low self-esteem. By contrast, her sister Joan gave a different meaning to the situation, believing that if she could survive this traumatic experience she could survive anything. She interpreted the situation to mean that she was strong and a survivor. Thus her life circumstances supported her belief that she was a capable and worthy human being. Same circumstances, different meanings, with different results.

We can use the same process in our everyday lives, choosing to give a different meaning to any circumstance, thus changing our behavior and attitude. I worked with a woman whose husband constantly complained and was very critical of her. For many years she believed everything he said and that she was a worthless person. This led to an endless cycle of attack and defend, with everyone involved feeling miserable. Then, after reading Dr. Jerry Jampolsky's book, *Love Is Letting Go of Fear,*[16] this woman decided to see each of her husband's attacks as a cry for love, since, as Dr. Jampolsky explains, underneath it all, love is what everyone really wants. Interpreting her husband's behavior in this new light, she was able to let his words pass by and see him as someone asking for love. As a result she was able to respond to him with love and patience rather than defense. Over time she not only transformed the situation but also greatly strengthened her own self-esteem by responding with love rather than anger. She did this by reframing the situation, thus giving new meaning to what she experienced.

Similarly if you are having a difficult interaction with someone you can ask yourself, "What can this person teach me about myself," thereby turning an antagonistic situation into an enlightening one. When something less than wonderful happens, first I let myself feel the feelings that the circumstance triggers. After I have allowed myself those feelings without judgment, I say to myself not only "What can I learn from this?" but also "What is a more positive meaning I can give to this beyond the immediate appearance?"

One particularly dramatic example occurred when I sold my sports medicine practice to an associate. One year later, after having made a small down payment, my associate backed out of the contract, telling me that he was not going to pay the balance and that he was opening his own office two miles away! Since there were numerous loopholes in the contract and I had already started another practice a thousand miles away, there was little I could do. Every penny my associate had promised to pay me was owed to other people who had loaned me money to start that practice. After flying back and forth, trying to salvage what I could of the situation, and simultaneously trying to get a new practice started, I became ill and finally collapsed.

From the depth of my illness came the reframe I was looking for. I had been asking myself, "What can I learn from this?" Sometimes when we ask ourselves that question there is a tendency to be cynical and say, "Never to do that again, that's for sure." We may also come up with some rather earthy, practical answers, which can be valuable. But the answer we are looking for to truly reframe the situation will give us a sense of peace and acceptance which helps us to move on.

Although I learned many practical lessons from this bad business deal, as well as many spiritual lessons including forgiveness, what allowed me to let go and ultimately move on was my ability to reframe the situation. Over the years I had read numerous success stories about millionaires and other highly successful people. A common denominator seemed to be that they had all failed or gone bankrupt at one time or another. Suddenly I felt that this was my ticket, my passport to success, since now I had lost big too. I reasoned that if I had lost big, I would also win big, if I could just totally accept what had happened and let it go.

So I dealt with the situation, paying back all my debts and slowly building myself up from there. Today, I consider myself far more successful in every aspect of my life than I was at that time. By reframing, I was able to give my circumstances new meaning so I could move forward more empowered than before.

We can wait and find a new meaning for something after we've let ourselves blame and suffer for a while, or we can feel the initial emotions and then say to ourselves, "It's time to move on," "How can I look at this to empower myself now?" "What can I learn from this?" or "What new meaning can I give this?"

Attitude of Gratitude

Gratitude is a quality of being incorporating acceptance and appreciation. An *attitude of gratitude* can work wonders to overcome negative states of mind. If you are in a low mood, daily repetitions of what you are grateful for will miraculously transform your feelings.

Having demands and expectations of people or life can keep you from feeling gratitude. You know you have a demand rather than a preference when you become angry or depressed as a result of that expectation not being met. In this painful or frustrating state of mind you are at the far end of the spectrum from a state of gratitude.

Have you ever met people who complain about everything? Have you ever noticed a part of yourself that often finds fault with things, people, or circumstances. I used to be like this much of the time. I call it the *never satisfied syndrome* and believe it is an offshoot of an active inner critic. I was accepting of other people's differences until it came to things related to me; then I always noticed what was wrong. There was a time when I would complain a lot about many little things, although I was oblivious to it, just as I had become used to my father always seeing what was wrong with things. Then one day a friend called my father's behavior to my attention. This friend and I had picked him up from the airport, and later she said to me, "Did you notice how your dad kept complaining about all the things you do (your car is too small, your house is too expensive, you're driving too fast) for most of the trip home?" I hadn't even noticed since I was so used to it, both from having grown up with this behavior and from having adopted it as my own internal language.

After this incident, I started to notice how much I voiced (both internally and out loud) my disgruntled attitude towards things and situations, eventually seeing it as an obnoxious behavior pattern. I realized how much unhappiness and loss of energy my holding the never satisfied syndrome caused me and committed myself to changing it. This was one of the hardest behavior patterns for me to change.

I began by noticing what I said out loud and sometimes just stopping myself in the middle of a sentence. After a while I stopped complaining out loud completely, although I still had the general feeling of being dissatisfied with life. Until I experienced a turning point. I had been feeling depressed and impatient that life or Spirit wasn't allowing me to discover my divine purpose and a friend said, "I used to feel the same way but then I started to be grateful for every opportunity to serve that Spirit put before me, however small it seemed, and trusted that this was fulfilling divine purpose." Suddenly I realized that I had many conditions and expectations about what fulfilling a purpose was supposed to look like, and if something didn't meet those criteria, then I was purposeless. I then realized that there were many things in my life I could choose to see as ways of fulfilling a divine purpose. I began to express gratitude for the many small day-to-day opportunities to serve and for all the blessings in my life.

An even more significant shift in my energy occurred when I decided to give gratitude every day for everything I could think of. At first this was a big stretch because I had been feeling low for quite some time, and it is hard to express gratitude when you are feeling badly. But I knew that I had a lot to be grateful for, whether I felt it or not, so I forced myself to express it out loud daily. As a result, the weight lifted and I started to notice how purposeful my life really was. I had needed to become more present and trust the process, instead of being ten steps ahead of myself, and the gratitude helped me do it. In retrospect, I can see how all past circumstances contributed to a great unfoldment. Now I feel exceedingly grateful for many things and all that I do feels purposeful. It is as if the more I am grateful, the more good things and circumstances are bestowed on me. Have you ever noticed how you enjoy giving more to people who seem genuinely grateful to receive your gift or service? I believe it is the same with Spirit.

To this day I say prayers of gratitude regularly, sometimes taking a long walk down the beach and expressing gratitude the entire time. Once you begin, it's amazing how many things you can think of to be grateful for. I don't find fault with too much anymore—undoubtedly a behavior change that has come, in large part, as a result of consistently acknowledging my gratitude.

TRY IT!

1 | Powerful Questions

❏ Make a commitment to catch your disempowering statements and questions (usually beginning with "why"), and change them to empowering expressions like, "What can I do in order to ___ (feel or have the thing you want)?" Focus on this for one week. If you like the new feelings you experience, extend the commitment one week at a time.

❏ Make a list of the things you want to have in your life, either in the form of qualities you would like to exhibit (such as patience, strength, compassion), or circumstances. Then form an empowering question about each one of these. For example, "What must I do, feel, know, or learn to have better health in my life?" or "What block can I become aware of and move through that will allow me to have the fullest relationships possible?" Hold the question, that is, regularly repeat the question until the answer appears in your life.

2 | Reframing

❏ Pick two or three situations that you are displeased with. Regarding each one, ask yourself, "What does this mean to me or about me?" Write the answers as quickly as possible to get your most immediate response.

❏ Take each situation and the responses you have just written and ask yourself, "What new, more empowering meaning can I give this? What important lesson or value can I learn from this?" Write the answers quickly without giving them too much thought.

3 | Cultivating an Attitude of Gratitude

❑ Take a day or two to listen to your internal dialogue and how you talk to others. Carry a piece of paper and make a check mark every time you complain about something or say something negative about yourself, others, or circumstances. See how many check marks you end up with. Do this for a longer period of time until you decide to let go of the "never satisfied syndrome."

❑ Make a list of everything you can think of for which you are grateful. At the top of the page write, "I am grateful for ___." Then quickly, without giving it a lot of thought, write the things that pop into your mind. To make this exercise even more powerful, have a friend do it with you. Face your friend and say, "I am grateful for ___." When you've completed, your friend can say, "Thank you for your gratitude." Then have your friend share with you what they are grateful for.

Read your list out loud at least once or twice every day. If you begin and end your day this way, you will be amazed at the positive feelings you will experience.

❑ Make another list. At the top of the page, write, "I am grateful for ___." This time list all the things you desire or are working toward. Empower the exercise by saying it out loud to a friend. Your friend can respond by saying, "You're welcome. It is yours. You deserve it."

When we are grateful for things before they occur, it seems to hasten their manifestation. Perhaps this is because the statement of gratitude affirms that something has already happened. Whatever the reason, gratitude in advance is another great way to work with affirmations.

Express Your Courageous
and Creative Self

THREE

PART

chapter thirteen

Taking Risks—
Standing in Your Truth and Setting Boundaries

Up to this point much of our discussion has pertained to inner work. Now is the time to focus our journey out into the world. In earlier chapters, we worked on gaining the trust of our inner being through the practices of inquiring within, listening, expressing and releasing, accepting our feelings, speaking kindly to ourselves, and other forms of nurturing behavior. As we do this work, the voice of our inner being becomes clearer and more specific about what it desires and what it wants to avoid.

To further increase the clarity of this inner voice and enhance the health of the inner being, it is necessary to take risks by doing new things, going against the norm, and standing up for ourselves. Such practices are essential to expressing ourselves and exploring more creative realms. The ongoing development of a trusting and loving relationship with ourselves gives us the courage to stretch and take more risks. Two other important factors contribute to our courage to take risks: standing in your truth and setting boundaries.

Standing in Your Truth

In previous chapters, we learned to hear our inner messages and to know what our truth is. Then we learned to honor our truth, by suspending our judgments and desire to talk ourselves out of it and finding ways to incorporate it into our lives. The next step is *standing in your truth*, that is, being willing to hold firm to what you believe is right and true for you even when challenged by others or difficult circumstances. The more you practice standing in your truth, the more your courage grows.

We have spent much of our lives acquiescing to the desires of others or conforming to their standards. We have learned to set aside our feelings and desires when they conflict with the expectations of family, friends, or society for fear of losing their approval or being left alone. In addition, we have been taught that to focus on our own desires is selfish and therefore bad. Consequently, any time we begin putting our desires first, or it looks like someone might be adversely affected by our actions, a reflex reaction occurs that either stops us from pursuing our choice or causes us great internal conflict. Awareness is are called for in such situations.

> *Once we become aware that we are basing our actions on the desires of others or the fear of their responses, we can then decide to make choices based on our own truth instead. In order to do this we must listen for our own desires and inner knowing and be willing to face the consequences when we act on our truth.*

Although there are times when standing in our truth will cause adverse consequences, there are many more times when the consequences are much less difficult than we imagined. We fear that people will dislike us, be mad at us, say bad things, or abandon us if we do what is right and true in our own hearts instead of what we think they would like. Sometimes our fears are justified, but often others are much more accepting than we think they will be or what occurs turns out not to be that bad in the long run. Survival fears also come up when we take risks that involve our source of livelihood, but more often than not I see the courage to make a leap of faith met by miracles that support that leap. I have also seen circumstances where an inner-directed change was resisted because it meant giving up a certain standard of living or letting go of some prized possessions. In such cases I ask the individuals, "Are you willing to give up your soul for your stuff?"

Whether the consequences are nonexistent or severe, there is an assurance that comes with standing in your truth. When decisions and actions are based on your inner knowledge, they ultimately work out for the better, because your inner being, with its direct link to your higher self, always knows what is best.

To stand in your truth, you first have to discover your truth by listening to your inner being. Sometimes the truth is not immediately apparent, especially when it comes to making decisions, because the mind gets caught up in weighing all the pros and cons of the situation. Making a decision with the mind alone can be difficult and often leaves you frozen, unable to move in any direction. I recommend allowing yourself to "be in the unknown." In other words, make it a practice to stop the back-and-forth thoughts relating to the pros and cons. After initially evaluating all the sides of the situation, calm your mind and let go of the issue. I find it helpful to stop such thoughts in midstream and say to myself, "I'll know when I know." I've had enough experience in this to have confidence that ultimately, the truest answer surfaces through either feelings or life circumstances. Particularly with large decisions, the mind will get you into a mental tennis game, slowly driving you crazy. Awareness and self-discipline are required to stop this bantering and allow the creative space of the unknown to guide you. This is where you get to practice surrender.

Another helpful tool in this process is the use of questions. Ask your higher self a specific question that will help guide you in the right direction. I usually say something like, "What is the highest truth in this situation and give me the strength to stand in this truth." Then I hold the question, periodically repeating it until eventually the answer is revealed. Although it sometimes takes a while for the answer to become clear, if you have cultivated your ability to be in the unknown this period does not have to be stressful.

The busy workings of the mind leave no room for messages from your inner being, while allowing yourself to be in the unknown will open space for the highest truth to come through. Things that cultivate this ability to be in the unknown are right brain activities, such as being in nature, art, music, song, dance, fun sports, exercise, or any form of play. Doing what nurtures you in times of stress can take discipline because sometimes the inner being shuts down and you don't feel like participating in enjoyable or nurturing activities. Just as it requires self-control to stop the internal dialogue about a decision, it takes self-management to stop what you're doing, however important it may seem, and do something enjoyable. Such activities get you out of your left-brain, linear mind and into your right-brain, creative mind, allowing your truth to become evident.

The process of standing in your truth often works like this. First you have a sense of knowing about what you are feeling, what you are to do, or how you are to be. This will happen through either subtle internal senses or life's circumstances showing you a direction. Once you have this sense of knowing, your ability to stand in your truth comes into play. Although you may have a good indication of what path to take, your fear of the immediate consequences can overpower any decision. This is where extra support from your higher self may be required. Asking daily for the strength to stand in your own truth can help you, even in the most challenging situations. Sometimes our own willpower or desire to improve our lot is just not enough to move us through a difficult situation. Prayer or asking our higher self for support on a regular basis will usually give us the extra strength necessary to face the fear of consequences for standing in our truth. The more times you move through this process, be it with simple or complex situations, the more your strength and courage will build.

When we take the risk to stand in our truth, we leave many knowns behind, and with them a sense of security. However, true security lies in our ability to tap into and be directed by our higher self, which we can access through our inner being. Therefore, the more we cultivate communication with our inner being which helps us know our truth, the more we can feel our connection to the higher source. And the more connected we feel, the more courage we have to take risks and face the consequences of our decisions. This doesn't mean we don't experience fear when taking risks, but we know that the consequences of our decisions are worth the price for the growth, joy, and enhanced self-expression that we ultimately gain from standing in our truth.

My Story of Standing in My Truth

A turning point in my ability to truly support my inner being and stand in my truth came shortly after the death of my father. I was scheduled to give a weekend seminar to a group of doctors. Giving these lectures was quite uncomfortable for me since the environment I had to be in and the image I believed I had to uphold felt rigid, which was opposite to my more creative nature. But the money was good and I had spent a long time cultivating the opportunity to be hired for such an honorable position.

Before my father's death, I had been flying frequently back and forth from Hawaii to California and Florida and had also been involved in numerous projects. After my dad died, however, I decided my incessant doing had to stop. I wanted space and time to feel my feelings about my dad's death and whatever else might surface. Consequently three or four weeks before the lecture was scheduled I called the head of the organization, a well-respected man in the profession who had believed in me enough to give me this opportunity, and I told him that my dad had died and was in no condition to stand before a group of doctors. He answered, "Well if it had happened the week before I would understand, but you have three weeks to get it together." Not wanting to cause problems, I backed down from my truth and agreed to show up.**

After another week, my inner being let me know that teaching this seminar was a big mistake. Every time I thought of it, I got a sick feeling in my stomach and felt tired and depressed. I had made time and space to allow my deeper feelings to surface, and my inner being was just beginning to reveal some hidden emotions to me. All the activity involved in preparing for the seminar, along with actually going to it, would surely interfere with my grieving process. Thus, my truth became glaringly clear—I could not go.

One of the most challenging acts of standing in my truth was calling the head of the organization and telling him I absolutely was not going to do it. My sense of responsibility to my worldly commitments has always been very important to me, so to back out seemed irresponsible. However, on another level, I knew I was

---

** It is very sad that this culture devalues the grieving process. After a loved one dies, we are expected to be back on the job three days later. By contrast, in some primitive cultures the community fully supports the bereaved for an entire year, taking care of them while they go through the healing process. Part of our emotional denial system comes from not being supported in grieving all the many losses that occur in our lives—including the loving childhood we may have never experienced, job losses, death of pets or loved ones, or any strong disappointments. It is sometimes difficult to fully move on because there is no permission or encouragement to take time to stop and feel our feelings associated with such losses.

finally being responsible to myself. My relationship with myself had often been put on the back burner for the sake of productivity, both worldly and domestic. It had always been important to take care of everything else but my deepest relationship with myself. Now I was proving to my inner being that I could be trusted to put myself first when necessary. Although I certainly don't advocate breaking agreements, sometimes when we are out of balance in one direction it takes overcompensating in the other direction to attain a healthy middle ground.

When I told the director I would not teach, he responded negatively as I had expected, reflecting my inner patriarchal voice that only valued productivity. However, I knew I had to stand strong for my truth, even in the face of his accusations and legal threats. I also had to stand up to my own inner critic, who wanted me to feel shame for being so irresponsible. I suddenly felt totally naked. One of the things I had held onto for my sense of value was being a respected, responsible, and productive individual. Now I was dropping this persona and accepting that my essential being was enough. I could love myself for just being, and not for what I did. On one level, I felt traumatized as I let go of my defense mechanism, while on another, I was very happy and felt a renewed sense of trust in myself.

Despite our fears, the repercussions of standing in our truth often don't amount to much. Not once have I stood firmly on an inner truth and not had it ultimately work out to the good of all—even in this case. A few weeks after the seminar was to have occurred, I checked back with the sponsoring college. The woman I spoke to was completely understanding and in addition said that canceling the event had saved the college money because enrollment had been very low. Consequently, I was able to improve my relationship with myself and help the sponsoring organization as well.

Although standing in our truth doesn't always end with everyone happy, it usually doesn't cause any real harm when the choice has been made from an inner truth and directed by a higher power. Other people involved may not approve of our choices, and even when things do work out the best for all concerned, they may never admit to it. Nevertheless, acting from our own authenticity is ultimately more valuable than gaining outer approval.

Setting Boundaries

As we practice being in our truth and standing on that truth, we begin to engage in a practice called *setting boundaries*. *Boundaries* is a term that is widely used and has many definitions depending on the orientation of those using it. Another commonly used term with a wide range of definitions is *codependence*. My interpretation of these two terms as they apply to the journey of truth is as follows.

Codependence is being dependent on another person's love or approval for a sense of self-worth. If we are codependent we won't risk doing anything we think might result in the withdrawal of that love or approval. We will do what we think will get it even if it goes against what is true for us. Another aspect of codependence is giving up what is true for us or otherwise altering our words and actions in order to avoid another person's reactions, or trying to protect them or ourselves from experiencing a particular feeling. In order to play the codependence game, we must ignore our inner voice, since it is the inner being that wants to tell us how to break free of the prison of codependence. We will also have a great aversion to feeling our deepest feelings, because being hooked in a codependent loop will help us avoid those feelings—that is, until the dam breaks and we find ourselves in a flood of feelings often equal to the intensity of the denial.

> *Codependence and boundaries go hand-in-hand, codependence being the culprit and boundaries the antidote. The way out of this cycle of codependence—internal numbing to explosion or breakdown—is through the practice of setting boundaries.*

In this context, setting boundaries means knowing your inner truth and then setting limits based on this truth. This might take the form of saying no to people when your tendency, though not your truth, is to say yes. Or it might involve setting limits on your own or others' behaviors that you find unacceptable, for example, a spouse's drinking. Although you may not be able to change the other's behavior, you can set a limit on how much of a particular behavior you will allow in your life.

When you set boundaries, there are often immediate repercussions. As you disrupt an old dynamic between two people, there is bound to be resistance. The other player will push every button they know to get you back to the old game plan, using such tactics as guilt, criticism, or emotional or physical abuse. Consequently, inner strength is required to maintain boundaries. Calling for divine assistance in such challenging circumstances can greatly empower you.

When one party of a codependent pair sets a boundary, the dynamic between them is altered. The other individual will either rise to the occasion, thereby raising their own level of awareness and growth, or the relationship will change. This is the risk you must be willing to take, for the codependent relationship protects both individuals from facing certain issues and feelings. If you have faced your issues and feelings and are willing to break out of the loop, either the other person will be forced to face their issues or, if they prefer to stay in denial, there may be a disruption in the relationship. It is the fear of this disruption that often keeps us from setting boundaries or standing in our truth. However, often this fear is unrealized and the other person responds to meet the challenge. At these times it is helpful to ask yourself the question, "Would I rather have the relationship the way it is and the apparent security or the life of my soul?"

> *Breaking out of a deeply codependent knot can be one of your greatest opportunities for spiritual mastery and can quickly catapult you to the next level of your inner journey. Although things may seem shaky or challenging while you are in this process, you can rest assured that if setting a particular boundary is inspired by inner knowing, the ultimate result will be a great expansion in your life.*

The earlier stages of this work are the changes we make within ourselves—how we talk to ourselves and how we treat ourselves. Setting boundaries for ourselves in relation to others is advanced work. To most effectively set our boundaries with others, we must have already cultivated a good deal of trust within ourselves, so our inner being trusts that our outer being will be there for it on all levels. This is not to say that you can't set boundaries with others before this occurs, but the ability to do so is enhanced greatly by a strong base of self trust. In addition, one action feeds and supports the other—setting boundaries helps to cultivate the trust of the inner being, which in turn strengthens the ability to set boundaries. A well-established relationship with our inner being makes challenging situations less stressful.

As you become more true to who you are in the world, you may find that your circle of friends changes. When you put out that which is other than who you truly are, you will attract those people who are aligned with that. As you begin to express yourself in a more authentic way, you will attract individuals who resonate with that, while those who cannot accept you as you are will fall away. Although this can be sad, remember that relationships approached from this more authentic place will ultimately be more satisfying. When we are consistent in taking care of ourselves, standing in our own truths, and setting boundaries, our relationships become richer, more intimate, and fulfilling.

TRY IT!

1 | Standing in Your Truth

❑ Write down the truth about three issues or circumstances that you have not yet expressed to a significant person or people in your life (or if you have expressed it, you have done nothing else about it).

❑ Ask yourself, "What is one step or action I can take to begin to express these truths?"

2 | Setting Boundaries

❑ Ask yourself, "What am I tolerating from others?" and "What can I do to begin to set a boundary regarding this?"

❑ Return to questions 1 and 2 periodically. If you have taken any of these steps and they feel right to you, ask yourself, "What is one more step I could take?"

fourteen

Changing Behavior— Seeking and Creating Balance

The last and critical step in the process of change is actually altering behavior. Through willingness, awareness, and insight, we open ourselves to what is not working for us, such as nonproductive behavior patterns, hidden feelings that plague us when they surface, or belief systems that run our lives. Once we have uncovered these keys and released the blocked energy associated with these patterns, then we can plant the seeds of change—new behaviors, which when fully integrated into our lives will make whatever changes we desire a permanent part of our reality. Alan Cohen, a popular author and workshop facilitator puts it this way, "If you always do what you've always done, you'll always get what you've always got." Therefore, if you want different results, do things differently.

As you approach this last stage of creating and instituting new behaviors in your daily life, it is helpful to restate your commitment to do whatever it takes to move forward in your life. Reaccess your willingness and motivation to make these changes. Acknowledge yourself for your willingness to feel uncomfortable feelings and to own some negative aspects of your being. Acknowledge how far you've come on the journey. Give yourself lots of credit, love, and support for what you have already accomplished before stepping out into the more treacherous waters of changing behavior.

Changing Behaviors

It is usually helpful to change a behavioral tendency by incorporating the counterbalancing opposite behavior into your life. For example, if you become aware that you have the tendency to play the helper role with a strong desire to fix people's problems, the counterbalancing behavior is to hold yourself back and do or say nothing the next time a friend discusses their problems. If you are typically a shy stay-at-home type of person but have discovered that a hidden aspect of you wants connection with people, a counterbalancing behavior may be to take a job working with people or commit yourself to talking to a new person every time you go out. If you are a person who doesn't like to take initiative, a counterbalancing behavior might be to find projects that require self-motivation or leadership, perhaps helping others with something you are good at. This will help you gain ability and trust in yourself to do things on your own. If you are workaholic, encourage yourself to take time off for fun, nurturing, or creative activities.

A man named Eddy used the concept of balance to help himself with a series of negative behavior patterns. He would frequently experience an angry reactionary response over little things such as when driving, small frustrations, or his own or other people's lack of perfection. He saw this as focusing on fear so to help himself move out of this fear place he would regularly chant to himself, "Love versus fear," thus shifting his attention to a more loving response. Over a period of time he was very successful in changing his previously negative responses.

As with learning any new skill, this process of learning a new behavior requires practice and focus until it becomes second nature. A warning—don't use changing behaviors as another opportunity to judge and berate yourself. It is vitally important to be easy on yourself and give yourself lots of room to fail. Use your understanding of the learning process, described below, to help you practice patience and self-acceptance.

The Learning Process—four stages for learning anything new:

1 | The first stage is *unconscious incompetence*. This is when you don't know that you don't know. In this stage learning or change in behavior is not possible.

2 | The second is *conscious incompetence*. This is when you know that you don't know. For example, you may know that you want a different result in a certain aspect of life and you become aware of your limiting beliefs. But you do not yet have the ability to change the beliefs or to take different actions. Although you can catch yourself saying things that you wouldn't have noticed before or perceive other limiting behaviors, you don't yet know how to change them.

3 | The third stage is *conscious competence*. This is when you are learning something new with intense concentration. You can start instituting a change, but it requires a good deal of attention to maintain the learning. At this step you may intermittently slip into the old pattern.

4 | The fourth stage is *unconscious competence*. This is when you just do something. You know you know, and you don't have to think about it any longer, such as when you have learned a skill so completely that thought is unnecessary. At this stage you find your life becoming a reflection of your new beliefs.

It takes time to learn anything new and you cannot expect to succeed instantly. The tendency is to think that once we have an awareness of a limiting belief and have put a new behavior into practice one time, we have mastered the change. When we revert to an old pattern, there is an underlying feeling of "you should have done better" or "there you go, you blew it again." I have never seen anyone fully break an old habit or institute a new behavior immediately, but it's as if we all expect ourselves to do so.

When you fall back into an old behavior, or repeat a pattern that you thought you had eliminated, be loving and gentle with yourself. Give yourself credit for just having the intention to change your behavior and know that any progress, however small a step it may seem, deserves positive acknowledgment. Your loving acceptance in such situations is an additional opportunity to enhance your relationship with your inner being.

You will soon find that the time from awareness of an old negative behavior to activation of a new, more empowered behavior gets shorter and shorter, until the process becomes natural. You will become unconsciously competent in your ability to practice the tools and to institute the new desired behaviors, and you will find the rewards well worth the effort.

Balancing the Opposites

Another important step on the journey that often involves changing behavior is cultivating balance. This means balancing extremes or smoothing out our unhealthy edges, and bringing them to a centered place of harmony and health. To do this, it is helpful to ask ourselves, "Does this belief, philosophy, behavior, or approach to life accentuate an imbalance I'm already experiencing or does it make me more centered and give me greater peace of mind?" Seeking balance can be something we do in any aspect of life. I will give you examples of several aspects of my life where the issue of balance has been significant.

As I moved along this path, I began to notice the existence of many paradoxes between different psycho-spiritual philosophies. One philosophy would seem to make sense, and at the same time it would appear to be negated by another philosophy that also felt right. For example, I believed in a philosophy that emphasized setting goals, writing them down, visualizing, then working hard. However, at the same time I was engaged in spiritual teachings that told me to surrender to the flow, let go and let God, don't push the waters, or just relax and it will all take care of itself. Since both philosophies made sense to me but were diametrically opposed, I felt confused.

After being upset by this confusion for awhile, I then found I was able to access what felt right about both of them, take the best of each, and integrate them. What rings true to me now is to plan for the future, set goals, visualize what I believe I want, and then let it go. Who knows, maybe there is something better for me than I even thought of. This requires letting go of my attachment to the outcome and being open to other possibilities. Of course, the more I am in tune with my feelings and my truth, the more appropriate these goals will be. Even so, there is still the possibility that they will not be for my ultimate good or that of those around me. So, while I am affirming these goals, I am also releasing my attachment to them and maintaining an openness to alternatives. This is the balance I found between those two philosophies.

Another place to balance that is similar to the paradox of the philosophies of goals versus surrender relates to how we actively live out those two dynamics in our work. One extreme is when people are unmotivated, put in minimal effort, and "live for Friday." The other extreme is when people work hard in a non-stop fashion because they feel they have to "push to make it happen." When we are out of balance on this end, we frequently experience burnout or find that we are ineffectively spinning our wheels without a lot to show for it, or we have a lot to show for it materially, but our relationships, health, or state of mind are suffering.

Finding balance with work is both an internal and external process. Internally, you need to commit strongly to an intention while simultaneously surrender. Externally, the balance manifests as working with energy and focus, then trusting that you'll get there when you get there by allowing time for creative and pleasurable activities.

A good balance, particularly if you work for yourself, is to work committedly at something, then step back a bit and let yourself be guided as to the next step. This also applies to the balance between work and play. When people say "I just can't afford to take time off," looking at the bigger picture, I often tell them they can't afford not to take time off. Success is not just how much money you make, it is also how happy and fulfilled you are in all aspects of your life. Unfortunately, people forget this when they put money blinders on and think that career and finances totally define success. Again, it's the balance.

Another area in which to cultivate balance is decision making—finding the balance between the head and the heart. Our best decisions come from a healthy combination of the two. Commonly we get confused about whether it is our head or our heart that is guiding us, thus making a choice can be a challenge. When we feel the subtle urging of the heart, our minds want to discourage what seem to be irrational actions. In this way our minds tend to keep us frozen, unable to act.

A good trick to discern the difference between messages coming from the head or heart is to ask yourself which one has a "should" in it. It is the head that communicates to us using "shoulds." The heart, or inner knowing, never speaks in terms of "shoulds" but instead prompts or gently urges us to do or not to do something. Although there may be valid concerns, the mind can help you evaluate which thoughts are worth considering and which are just old limiting beliefs unnecessarily holding you back. Once you uncover the "shoulds," you can ask your higher self to assist you in how best to come to a resolution. This process of discernment by separating out the shoulds then bringing in prayer, will help you attain more balance between the head and the heart.

Much of the process of achieving balance is about balancing the yin (non-linear, heart-centered, feminine) and yang (logical, rational, masculine) aspects of our natures. This is reflected in what I have already mentioned such as making decisions from the head or the heart and approaching our lives through control or through surrender. We also see this yin/yang issue in our tendency to "do" compulsively versus the ability to be comfortable with just being, in isolating versus connecting, in being fixed about things versus the ability to be flexible.

Another type of balance associated with yin and yang energy is coming from feelings versus working with our minds. I am referring here to how we approach life in general. If we live mostly in our heads, spending much of our time mentally processing things, we diminish our capacity to access our emotions and subtle feelings. When this is the case, feelings tend to emerge as an expression of overload—with crisis points and periodic blowups. The swing will be from no feelings to excess emotion, sometimes along with destructive behaviors. An extreme version of this is the quiet, mild-mannered guy in the back office who turns out to be a killer. At the other end of the spectrum is the individual who is excessively emotional, overreacting to things that appear insignificant.

Achieving balance between working with our emotions and with our minds is an important step for positive change.

> *Although being able to feel our feelings is an extremely important part of knowing our truth and being a whole and passionate being, the ability to balance this by using our minds effectively is equally important.*

We can master our self-talk so that our feelings do not run past their point of true expression. A pure feeling does not last that long. We extend it with our resistance to it or the circumstances. Thus, using the mind to help the emotional expression come to completion is a good balance.

Working with the mind can also help us to transform our belief systems, change our self-talk from critical to accepting, and shift our perspective about something—reframing. Although making these transitions in the mind is essential, working only with the mind can result in denial of the emotions. We must fully feel and release the underlying emotion before we use the mind to help us transform our thought and action patterns. Consequently, both feeling and thinking need to be integrated into our growth process.

The key to achieving integration of all these different opposites is to avoid judging yourself for being too much one way or another and simply notice any imbalance. Then consciously work with your behaviors until you achieve a balance. It is often helpful to try an opposite mode for a while as a counterbalance, which will eventually bring you to a middle ground.

In our attempt to balance ourselves, it is essential that we make an honest assessment of who we are and what we put forth. One aspect of this is to look at the personas you use and to reevaluate them (see Chapter 7). If you can get honest with yourself and own the personas you wear, they can be focal points for choosing new behaviors.

The greatest benefit of taking the time, energy, and focus to balance your opposites and change behaviors is a heightened sense of spontaneity, creativity, and aliveness.

As we become true to ourselves, life becomes true to us. Being true to ourselves evolves from a practice to a way of life, and expressing who we are becomes easy and natural. We are then living an authentic life.

TRY IT!

1 | Inventory of patterns and tendencies

Use the list below as a guide to isolate your behavioral tendencies and habitual patterns, then add anything else you are aware of. Make a list of any tendencies that seem fixed or heavily weighted to one side or the other.

❑ Self initiative and action orientation
  ❑ Are you self-motivated to take action, or do you need outside influences?

  ❑ Do you consider yourself a do-er or a couch potato?

  ❑ Do you find that you rarely sit still and there is always something to do, or do you sit around a lot, reading, watching TV, relaxing, and doing very little?

  ❑ Are you a compulsive "do-it-nower," or do you prefer to procrastinate?

❑ Relationship to others
  ❑ Do you spend much of your free time with others, or alone?

  ❑ Do you enjoy being with people, or feel more comfortable alone?

  ❑ Do you tend to be very open with others, or closed and cautious?

  ❑ In a relationship, do you prefer to be with the other person most of the time, or tend to want independence?

- Do you experience ease with and enjoy intimacy, or tend to want distance?

- Do you often take care of or help others, or do others take care of you?

- Are you the initiator in connecting with people, or the receptive one, waiting for others to step forward?

- Are you very talkative, or quiet and shy?

- Do you reach out, or hold back?

❑ Material world
- Are you fastidious, or comfortable in messiness?

- Are you always the capable one, taking care of business, or do you need others to handle things?

- Do you collect possessions, or do you have few?

- Do you spend money with little regard, or pay attention to every penny?

- Do you believe only spiritual things matter and shy away from material possessions, or are you very attached to your possessions?

❑ Modes of operation
- Do you easily access and focus on your emotions, or are you rational about most things?

- Do you express your feelings a lot, or prefer to keep them to yourself?

- Do you act on impulse, or think things through before taking action?

❑ Are you usually optimistic and overlook the downside of things, or do you usually see what is wrong or why something won't work?

❑ Are you overly trusting, or overly cautious?

❑ Do you talk, eat, and move quickly, or do you move slowly?

❑ Do you spend a lot of time in your head, thinking about the future, planning, or worrying, or do you spend excessive time in your emotions easily upset or feeling anger, etc.?

❑ Do you complain a lot, or are you constantly cheerful?

❑ Do you frequently put others needs and desires before yours, or do you tend to think of your needs first?

❑ Do you work all the time taking little time for play, or do you play all the time and find it hard to stay focused?

2 | Counterbalancing

❑ Look at your list of key tendencies from #1 and think about what personas you most often assume (see Chapter 7 for ideas).

❑ With these in mind, write answers to the following questions:
❑ How does this tendency or persona cause problems or hinder you?

❑ How does it affect the quality of your relationships?

❑ What new behavior will help you change this pattern? If this appears to be a large undertaking, ask: "What is the first step I can take that will initiate such a change?"

chapter fifteen

Creatively Expressing—
The Joy of the Journey

After embarking on the journey to peel away the layers of what stands between you and your authentic self, there comes a point where you naturally desire to express in more playful and creative ways. For some this desire surfaces prior to beginning the journey but remains an idle dream, while others may already be involved in something creative. But most commonly we tend to hold back on the expression of our creative selves because expressing this way is associated with our more naked, exposed or authentic selves. Until one becomes comfortable with being and expressing that authentic self, the urge to express in more creative ways often does not even surface. If it does, then usually arising with it are a barrage of reasons why that urge should not be followed. This changes after having spent some time engaging in the work described in this book. Not only does the resistance fall away, but expressing creatively begins to feel like the best next step. At that point the work is to have fun. When you engage in the creatively expressive aspects of this path, all other work seems easier.

What does it mean to creatively express? My definition is: to set an intention to create something, then to get out of the way so that a higher force can join with you for something magical to be born. It is a triad—you, Spirit, and the medium—with Spirit expressing through you via the medium. The medium can be anything from what is usually considered an art form, such as music, painting, or dance, to a business or service project.

We provide a greater opportunity for this creative energy to come through us by doing our worldly work—by practicing, gaining experience, and so forth, so that this energy has more freedom to create through its vehicle of expression—you. It is also possible for this creative energy to express through you without skill or experience on your part. You only need to get your mind out of the way and refrain from judging the product or outcome. However, you can experience the most creative freedom by finding a balance between structure and no structure. When there is enough structure so that you are not struggling with basic capabilities, you can be more fully in the moment and feel the spirit working through you.

I asked an artist friend of mine his definition of creativity. He said, "My measure of creativity is how much you become absorbed in the process, so that you become one with the medium through which you are creating." This is being fully present, and when you are fully present, every moment is a creative moment. In athletics they refer to it as being "in the zone." Though this level of absorption is not a criterion for creativity, it does facilitate the manifestation of what you are creating. Paradoxically, creating is not about the result, it's about the process. While skill and expertise help, they do not always assure creativity. Many accomplished artists, musicians, and writers at times loose the in-the-moment fresh expression and with it the joy in their art form. At such times their art may be reduced to mechanical replications that rely on repetition of past successes. Their skill allows them to produce something that is acceptable by society's standards, but lacks soul, depth, and the ability to touch either the artist or the viewer. I have experienced audiences moved to their core by beginners who wrote and sang their own songs, which emerged from their unskilled center of creativity. Free will is also part of creativity.

> *When have to replaces want to or love to, an important element for creativity is lost. Creativity is not about performing or producing. It is about surrendering to the spirit of it. Then something powerful and beautiful can result, especially if you learn not to judge by worldly standards.*

Our judgments and expectations cause us to lose our capacity for spontaneous creativity. They make it difficult to experience the presence and unknown of the moment, where the truly creative is born. Often we don't know how to surrender to the emptiness and openness of the moment, where the magic occurs. We become attached to an outcome and fear that we will not meet the idealized standards of ourselves or others. Such attachment and fear close off the flow of creativity. Even if we manage to open up long enough to let something happen, we often judge the outcome as not good enough. Learning to disarm our inner critic (as discussed in Chapter 8) is essential to creativity.

Creativity can come through any activity, such as sports, daily chores, work, or social projects. Though creativity can be expressed in any area of life, I refer here mainly to artistic forms of expression. This is because being creative is about learning to fully surrender to the moment and any right-brain activity is good practice for this. The right brain is said to be the creative, nonlinear side of our brain, and expressing yourself through any art form draws upon the right brain. Although the fullest expression of our creativity will usually come from combined use of both sides, we are generally over accustomed to working with the left, linear, logical side of our brains and almost excluding the right. If we engage in activities that more specifically focus on the right, creative side of the brain, we can then bring the skill of working more creatively to anything else we do, even things that we might not normally consider creative.

As part of your program for cultivating a more creative life pick any art form and begin playing with it. Not only does this exercise right brain function, it exercises your capacity for creativity by allowing you to spend more time fully absorbed in something out of sheer joy, *not* because you have to. Most individuals are attracted to some art form, whether it is music, dance, painting, writing, or singing. But the rules and judgments that we apply to other aspects of our lives, we also apply to these arts. So we either stopped such activities at an early age or never started. If we did start but were not "good enough" to be in the upper ranks or make a career of it, chances are we were not encouraged to continue. Even if we were encouraged, our own comparisons and self-appraisals got in the way. Thus we end up leading "responsible" adult lives with very few avenues for creative expression. You can notice the tendency that keeps you from starting or continuing to do something creative but not let it stop you from making any small first step.

In most indigenous community-based cultures, communal creative expression is a natural way of life. In such societies, ritual—another right brain activity—is commonly performed. Singing, dancing, rhythm making, praying, or creating art together are regular aspects of community life. There are remnants of this in our culture, such as singing in church, but as people become disillusioned with more dogmatic forms of expressing spirituality, even this is diminishing. Communal expression also happens in a distorted form in bars—drinking and sometimes dancing; it is not surprising that alcohol and drug abuse are rampant. Watching sports provides another community ritual but does not provide creative expression for the observers. In our society there are few other means for creatively and communally channeling the tension and stresses of daily living. Moreover, the stress is enhanced when there are so many rules and mandates on our behavior and few outlets for healthy release through creative self expression.

A number of different programs exist for inner-city and at-risk teenage youth involving art or wilderness rites of passage. These programs have a high success rate in changing the attitudes and lifestyles of the participants. From this we can assume there is great potential for dealing with social problems by making expression through the arts and ritual a more available and normal part of our culture, including our personal lives.

In my workshops I find that most participants have experienced some specific suppression of their innate instincts towards artistic or creative endeavors. For example, some loved to sing when they were children and then were told "keep your voice down, you can't sing." Others loved art projects but were told not to make messes, or they thought their pieces were not as good as others. Some loved to dance but were told they had "two left feet." A common story I have heard is of women who love rhythm and wanted to drum when younger—but drumming was taboo for girls. There are stories of individuals who were forced to take piano lessons from an uninspiring teacher who didn't know how to make it fun, causing them to lose any desire to ever really learn to play. Consequently, they dropped the exploration of music, except to listen to what others create, and to harbor a seemingly futile longing to make music themselves. There are similar stories of jokesters with natural propensities for wit and humor who never even thought about cultivating it by taking an improv class or writing comedy. There are tales of frustrated poets who on rare occasions put something heartfelt on paper, only to be stuffed in a trunk.

This sentiment was exemplified when one man said, "I don't know if I will continue writing because I don't know if I am a writer." This is very sad. Of course he is a writer, just as I am a singer, and someone else is a dancer or poet—perhaps not in the eyes of our culture with its narrow standard of what is acceptable artistic expression. Consequently, there is not much expression, except by the limited few who meet the standards. Even those who are trying as hard as they can to meet society's standards, often lose their personal sense of expression in the process.

One woman told me that her child had been raised on creative expression. Having gone to a Waldorf school, where artistic expression is incorporated into the learning process, her daughter is very much in touch with her inner guidance and ability to express herself through art. She said that her daughter's nighttime dreams often show her exactly what to paint, and she follows this guidance—most of us have not been so fortunate.

What can we do about this? There are many possibilities for artistic creative expression. The key is to pick anything that catches your fancy even if you're not sure you want to focus on it for a long time. Trust your intuition and just begin—no matter how unskilled you may seem by worldly standards.

The important thing to remember is, creative expression is about the process, not the product!

This is a difficult thing to grasp in our society, where everything is rated according to performance, ability, appearances, and so forth—a source of much unhappiness for many people. I have heard countless stories and have my own experience of how relaxed, satisfied, and joyful I feel after a few hours of one of my favorite right brain activities—no matter what other challenging or upsetting events are occurring. The attitude that "If you don't do it great, don't do it" has many people stuck in unsatisfying left-brain life ruts. I suppose from the viewpoint of wanting to manage society it makes sense to keep the expressive arts for just the "talented few," since when people become too expressive, creative, and independent, they become harder to control. Most of us have bought the propaganda about doing something for the product rather than the process. Sadly, this belief keeps many people from ever even beginning to express themselves creatively, and we *all* have the capability within us.

In the workshops I facilitate, some of what we do is play with improvisational singing, rhythm, movement, and words. At first this seems intimidating due to people's preconceived ideas of how they believe they are supposed to perform. But it is exciting to see each person set aside their internal critic and just go for it. What emerges is an aliveness, playfulness, and spontaneity that actually produces some amazing results. Everyone is astounded by their innate capability to create when the pressure of judgment and "supposed to be's" is lifted. In the midst of expressing and playing within a safe space, deeper truths begin to emerge easily and spontaneously without much effort. It is beautiful to see how a profound awareness and shift can occur in the midst of having fun. Afterwards, the participants always feel vitalized, transformed and inspired. Moreover, once they have had the experience of suspending self-judgment so that something creative can come through, and of responding to the magic of the moment, they have a point of reference for doing this at work, home, or other places. They understand that they are in fact creative and can apply this creativity to anything they do.

If you can't think of what you would like to focus on for creative expression, a great place to start is with the voice. *Toning*—making long tones with the vowel sounds, which can be done from a low to high pitch—is easy and has an amazing effect on the nervous system. Many studies have shown that it actually *charges the brain*, energizing it and at the same time relaxing both the brain and body.

The positive effects of toning are exemplified in this story. A doctor named Alfred Tomatos was called upon to help a Benedictine monastery in trouble. All monks who had been used to working long and hard with high energy on four or less hours of sleep a night, had become lethargic or ill. As part of a modernization program, the new head of the order had dropped the Gregorian chanting—in which they sang long vowel tones—from their daily routine because he saw no need for it. When he noticed the unexplained condition of the monks, he brought in many different specialists to determine the cause. One said it was their diet. They had been strict vegetarians, so the recommendation was that they eat a heavy protein and meat diet. This succeeded only in slowing them down and depressing them more. After many unsuccessful attempts by different doctors to diagnose and solve the problem, Dr. Tomatos was brought in. After studying this situation, he immediately put the monks back on their original lighter diets and the rigorous routine of Gregorian chants that had been followed for centuries. Within six months every one of the monks was back to his old high-energy routine and free of illness. A few other monasteries adopted this same program, and most of the monasteries that did not return to chanting ultimately closed.

Toning is not only a powerful tool for the body and brain. It also releases emotional tension and opens blocked energy in the area of the throat, which is essential for expressing ourselves, be it speaking our truth or other forms of expression. In her book *The Healing Voice,* Joy Gardener provides instruction on how to do basic toning, as well as on the use of toning for emotional release. You can start with the basic vowels and from there begin to play, voicing whatever sounds come forth. I highly recommend including toning in your expressive arts regime, along with whatever else you choose to do. Another advantage is that it's easy, it's free, and it can be done anywhere. The car is a great place to tone because of the privacy we have there and how much time we spend driving.

Toning is just one of the many possibilities for creative expression, others are: taking a tap dance class, Afro dance class, or drum class, joining a chorus, sketching, painting, sculpturing, photography, creative writing, acting, or doing improvisational comedy. At forty-four, my sister took up ice skating. I know a women in her sixties in an Afro dance class, and many other people have started to learn new skills in their seventies or older. (I highly recommend the book *Growing Old Is Not for Sissies—Portraits of Senior Athletes* by Etta Clark). It is never too late to start. Private lessons are great, but there is something wonderful about learning a skill with others who also enjoy doing it.

Personally I love to sing and was a closet car singer for years. Because I couldn't sing perfectly on pitch, I never sang in front of anyone. Actually, I didn't sing much at all except on long trips in the car. Tears would roll down my face when I would hear certain singers perform because I would think, "That's me, I'm supposed to be able to do that! I got a bum deal and wasn't born with the pipes." At different points over the years, I have taken singing lessons but quit because it didn't seem like I was improving. I had been hung up on results but finally decided to accept my voice the way it was and just enjoy my singing, whatever came out. With this new perspective I have come to enjoy the process instead of waiting for perfection. Because of this, my voice is truly beginning to open up. Even though it's not the quality of a recording star, I don't care. I'm having fun with it and expressing myself with my own songs and sounds. After becoming more playful, putting less pressure on myself, and being willing to be seen without being perfect, my voice began to open up even more. Now I am leading song circles, participating in an improvisational accapella singing group, and am doing solo performances of songs I have written. This to me is a miracle, not only because I have come so far with it but because of the great joy it brings me. in addition, the opening that transpired with singing crossed over into many other areas of my life.

I encourage you from my heart to begin some creative endeavor. Letting go of your judgment may be the most difficult part, even more challenging than learning the skill itself. If you can let go of the judgment, however, not only will you enjoy yourself tremendously, but you may even discover you have a great deal more talent than you realize. I was in a singing performance class where a woman had gotten up to sing her piece. You could see this woman judging herself when she would make sounds she felt were not beautiful in her attempt to go for it in the way the teacher was suggesting. But after she received the feedback that we could see her judgments holding her back, she decided to let go and not worry about what it sounded like. As a result her singing became not only powerful but beautiful and expressive. When you attempt creative expression, it doesn't matter if you call what happens talent or not. What matters is that you let go of your idealistic expectations and allow yourself to get lost in the moment. Though there may be times when it seems difficult or scary to persist, there is a part of you that will leave the experience satisfied, fulfilled, and genuinely happy.

What most people report is that the satisfaction derived through creative efforts spill over to other areas of life, allowing even humdrum work to be performed with more enthusiasm. Your inner happiness will transform any experience. There are other benefits as well. The teacher of the singing class I mentioned noticed an interesting by-product of her class. She told us that many woman reported to her that they had lost weight while taking her class—without even trying. Apparently, something had happened to their psyches that had caused a shift, through letting their voices be heard and through their willingness to be seen nonjudgmentally by themselves and others. The more opportunities you give yourself to express creatively and focus on the process rather than the product, the happier you will be.

At one point I was an aspiring dancer, struggling in New York City to make it professionally. Then I suddenly became aware that as much as I loved to dance somehow all the fun had gone out of it. The joyful experience of dancing for its own sake was no longer there. Drained and exhausted, I decided to quit. Now when I dance it's just for fun—improvisational and creative with no rigid standards to meet. As a result I can let go into it, and am charged by it.

Another reason why creative expression can be so healing and balancing is that as we get extremely absorbed in the moment and in the process, we often go into what some describe as a *trance*, losing ourselves and functioning from a more primal portion of the brain. Indigenous cultures have used trances for eons because of their healing and balancing properties and, perhaps more important, their ability to create a deeper connection to life and Spirit. A trance is most commonly induced by repetitive actions, particularly with sound, such as chanting, singing, drumming, playing special instruments, and dancing. These forms of expressive arts are particularly therapeutic, but I believe most any form done with full focus can induce a healing trance state, especially when we no longer have to use our left brain to perform the activity. When we let go of our linear thinking and move into the moment this way, we access a connection that brings us ever closer to a state of peace and balance.

One of the beauties of the trance state is that it is healing to the body, psyche and emotions. Dr. Stan Grof, the originator of Holotrophic Breathwork, has done considerable research on the trance state for over thirty years. He says that the body has an organic desire to heal and bring itself into balance, and when it is in a naturally induced altered state this healing will automatically occur.

Another benefit of a trance state is that when intention is added to it, the trance will intensify the intention. For example, if you affirm your intention to heal a certain part of your body or to be free of a certain limiting pattern, and you state this intention just prior to going into a trance or during the trance, amazing miracles often result—particularly if you repeat the experience on a number of different occasions. Rituals make use of this concept by inducing a trance through sounds, smells, candles, special setting, and invocation; then intention is set with prayer, singing, or proclamation.

The benefits of committing yourself to a program of creative expression are numerous. This is one of the most enjoyable aspects of the journey, and since lightheartedness is an important attribute of an enlightened, happy, and whole individual, you might as well start working on this fun part now. Even making a commitment to creative expression for just a few hours one day a week will greatly support you on the rest of the journey. It can help give you self-confidence, inspiration, strength, and an optimistic outlook that will support you in other challenges that you may face. When you become more expressive in one area of your life it will carry over to other areas. Pretty soon you will find it easier to express your truth and feelings to others. Ultimately, this leads to more personal power, which not only helps you to express your personal truth but allows you to take the risks involved in expressing that truth. Expressing your truth as well as your creativity enhances enthusiasm and motivation, which helps you go for what you want in life. It is a self-supporting cycle. After a while your whole life becomes more of an expression of who you are, including what you put out into the world.

Bringing any one or more art forms alive in your life, whatever your level of expertise, together with learning to express your truth, is a winning combination for creating a more fulfilling, passionate, and expressive life.

TRY IT!

1 | List one to three forms of expression that you are strongly attracted to but have never done or rarely do.

2 | Using each of the answers to number 1, fill in the blank, and answer the question:
   ❏ When did I stop ____?

   ❏ Who silenced me or stopped me from doing ____?

   ❏ What was I scared of?

   ❏ What do I believe to be true about me in relation to ____?

   ❏ Is this really true?

   ❏ What would it take for me to start ____ or expand upon what I do now?

   ❏ Do I see taking care of myself in this way important enough to make this a priority and even give something else up if necessary?

3 | Pick one form of creative expression. Make a commitment to begin on a small scale and to follow through at least once a week. Try this for one month and see how it feels. Extend this if you like the results.

Transitioning to Right Livelihood

As you spend more time living in your truth—honoring your feelings, expressing what is real for you, and taking necessary risks—it is not uncommon to reach a point where you desire to change jobs or careers. Doing work that expresses the truth of who you are and what you love in a way that serves, I call *right livelihood*. I always get excited when I hear that someone is embarking on this stage of the journey because I believe so strongly that it is natural and our human right to find joy in how we express ourselves in the world. The message we have often been taught is that we have our work life, which is often boring or stressful, and then we have the rest of our life, which by virtue of it not being work, is supposed to be great. But this is not always the reality, because the unfulfillment from work can carry over into the rest of your life or vice-versa. I am not saying that our inherent happiness depends on what we do for a living, since part of the journey is to discover peace and fulfillment wherever we find ourselves. However, when we are expressing aspects of who we are through our work, life is more fun and fulfilling. It seems there is a natural progression on this path, that after you have spent some time working on yourself and your issues, a natural desire to serve others begins to develop. This is why I also call right livelihood doing your *service work*. Although service does not necessarily mean what you do for a living, I am referring here to your main area of worldly focus being of service, whether you receive monetary benefit or not.

There are many different ways to go about making this transition to expressive work. If you are one of the fortunate people who already love your work and feel fulfilled in it, you are probably not interested in making a change. But if you are one of the majority who feel stuck, it is important to consider this option.

As with everything else, it starts with your willingness and a clear decision that you want to make a career or job change or express through a creative project. If this is true, realize that it might create challenges ahead, but take comfort in knowing it is something that your inner guidance has indicated is right for you. At this point, you do not have to know either exactly what you will be doing or how you will make this change on a practical level. However, this is also the point where most people get stuck—in the unknown. Because they do not have a clear image of what they want or assurance about how things will turn out, numerous individuals give up before they start, saying, "I just can't" or "I will when the next job is waiting for me." A common story seems to be, "I would love to get out of this job, but for financial reasons I can't." Although such a view has a basis in cold reality, there are other possibilities of what can happen if you hold a strong intention and are open-minded.

We all know, there are no guarantees in life, but many wonderful things happen when we take risks and are willing to work hard. They can also occur through "grace"—those miraculous opportunities that are bestowed upon us by Spirit, though I sometimes believe these are life rewards for other good work we have done. Whatever actually constitutes grace, the problem is that many people wait for such miraculous opportunities, never taking action and remaining dissatisfied in a place of perceived security.

Practicing the art of being in the unknown gives you the tool you need for the first step, which is to make a strong statement to yourself and to Spirit that you are ready and willing to make this change, regardless of the fact that you may not know what it is or how you will get there. You simply know that doing what you are doing no longer serves you and is not allowing you to use your talents to serve others. This can be a motivating factor to support your willingness to change, which begins with your ability to be in the unknown, without having to know the answers right away.

After you have made a decision to move toward right livelihood and have expressed your willingness to yourself and the forces at work. What is next? If you have no idea what you want to do, start by reading books like *What Color is My Parachute* by Richard Bowles, *Do What You Love and the Money Will Follow* by Marsha Sinetar, or one that has many great exercises to help you discover what you want, *I Could Do Anything If I Only Knew What it Was* by Barbara Sher. This book helped me see that giving up on my dream came from my fear and the deep programming that I had to put financial security above all else, including the fulfillment of my soul and joyful self-expression. After reading and doing the exercises in the book, I was able to renew my vision and again follow my dream. Reading books on the subject can inspire you, help you choose, or as was the case with me, get you back on course.

As you begin to get some clarity, even if you still do not know exactly what the picture will look like or how long it will take, it is time to take some steps, without worrying about being on exactly the right path. The point is to begin to put energy in motion. If you are going down path A with a good deal of energy, but it turns out not to be the path for you, all is not wasted. Eventually path B will emerge and you will have the momentum already going to move you down that path. You may have to follow side roads with twists and curves until you get to the highway that is taking you where you want to go. Do not think you are wasting your time, energy, or resources. You are putting energy in the energy bank. All your efforts and energy will have a bearing on your original intention, which is to do work that is the best expression of you. By contrast, if you never make the investment necessary to get started, you will never be anywhere other than where you are. So your willingness to apply some energy and effort—not struggle—in any direction that you are initially motivated is an important step. The process is this:

1 | access your strong willingness to make a change,
2 | research a direction for that change, and
3 | take some action steps however small or large, even if you only have a general direction.

These action steps might mean enrolling in some evening community education classes that teach you more about your subject of interest. If you have special skills, you might do community service or offer to teach a class. To learn more you could volunteer someplace that focuses on things of interest to you. You don't have to give up your job or do anything rash to begin to making the change—just start somewhere and trust the process.

As you start taking action, you will notice that you are gradually receiving greater clarity about your course. As the pieces of the puzzle begin to fit together, more specific planning becomes appropriate. However, do not be too attached to any plan because even though you may begin to take larger steps, the course is still subject to change.

This is a good time to start planning for the money you will need to comfortably make the transition. Whether you need time for a job search or for starting something of your own, always plan for longer than you think it will take. Even if you do not know exactly what you want to do yet, you can still start saving or planning for how you can acquire the funds to allow you to be without income for a while. This might require seeing where you can cut your expenses and starting to save little by little. Even if it looks like it will take five years to save up enough money for the transition, demonstrating your commitment to the change will often set forces in motion that can make miracles occur. The change will often happen much faster than you think, and even if it does take a long time, the act of moving towards the change will bring a new spirit of joy and enthusiasm into your life that can make even drudgery seem easier.

Doing Whatever it Takes

There will come a time when you are certain about what you want to do and you have begun to prepare financially for the transition. As you reach this point, you will need to make a bigger commitment—the commitment to *do whatever it takes*. On the path of truth, this can mean facing all the issues that are standing in the way of manifesting what you want. In the case of transitioning to right livelihood, it also refers to taking action which may require doing something you have never done before which may be scary or involve considerable energy output or risk. It is the commitment to this that will lead you where you need to go and make miracles happen. The famous quote by W. Murry says it well:

> Until one is committed there is hesitancy, the chance to draw back, always ineffectiveness. Concerning all acts of initiative (and creation) there is one elementary truth, the ignorance of which kills countless ideas and splendid plans: that the moment one definitely commits oneself, then Providence moves, too. All sorts of things occur to

help one that would otherwise never have occurred. A whole stream of events issues from the decision, raising in one's favor all manner of unforeseen incidents and meetings and material assistance, which no person could have dreamt would have come their way. I have learned a deep respect for one of Goethe's couplets: "Whatever you can do, or dream you can, begin it. Boldness has genius, power and magic in it."[17]

Because I have owned my own businesses since I was twenty-five, I have many personal stories of risk-taking and doing whatever it takes to start something new. One of these stories is about how I got started leading retreats and workshops. I knew I wanted to lead experiential, growth-oriented classes, but I had no idea what would be involved or where the people would come from. The odds seemed against me; I had never done this before, I was an unknown in this field and I did not have a Ph.D. at the time. Nevertheless, I set an intention to do this, even though I had no idea how to begin. Soon after, a friend approached me about forming a women's group. We decided that a different woman would facilitate each time. This friend and I decided to co-create one of the evenings, and as we began to work on it we realized that between us we had so many ideas that we ended up creating two different one-day workshops. To get started, we offered these first classes on a donation basis.

Doing something for the first time often requires considerable stretching and risk. Once I was over the first-time hump, I proceeded to create other opportunities for myself, offering my services in this way wherever possible.

Eventually, I became more comfortable with such workshops and decided to do a week-long retreat in a natural setting in Maui, where I had experienced so much healing myself. This time I teamed up with another woman, who was not only a good teacher but a networker as well. As it turned out, I had only a partial commitment to do this, which is equal to no real commitment at all. I realized later that I was leaning on her to fill the retreat, and though I did a share of marketing efforts, I did not do anything out of my comfort zone to market our retreat. She also had not truly committed herself since she had too many other activities going. Consequently, our efforts led to nothing. Only one person registered.

This was a turning point for me. I was either going to let this "failure" defeat me or use it to give me greater determination. After a few days of deliberation, I was ready for a big shift. I told myself and Spirit resolutely, "I will do whatever it takes, just show me what to do." After that, miracles started to happen. First, the retreat center that I was going to use decided to give me a second chance, even though they lost money when I canceled the original retreat and there was nothing to make them think I could make it happen on a second try. Next, by a series of serendipitous events I connected with a very talented man who had been leading workshops for quite a while and had a following. We had mutually supporting strengths and very similar paths, so decided to team up. I then met a woman who had done marketing for a man who was very successful with his seminars and hired her for a few consultations. Spending some money on people who have successfully done what you want to do can prevent wasted learning time and mistakes. I was so committed to making this dream a reality that I even moved to a more conducive location. Then, armed with a few good ideas and the willingness to put out a lot of energy, I proceeded to pound the pavement to fill the workshops we had set up in our area. Less than one year after making the firm commitment to myself "to do whatever it takes," we had an extremely successful retreat, not only in terms of the results for the participants but in terms of the number who came. This could be taken as a miracle, since neither of us was very well known, at the time I did not have much experience, and the participants were required to invest quite a bit of time and money. We put on these retreats for a number of years. They continued to get even better, and I continued to grow in my abilities.

In the beginning I did not know how my general vision of facilitating workshops would be manifested, since I did not have much experience in the field and it would involve a lot of financial risk. However when I reached a point where I was able to devote my full time to it and maintained the commitment "to do whatever it takes," then it manifested. A number of other prior projects I had started followed a course similar to the retreats. Sometimes I had to spend a long time making a living at something less desirable while I was working on the new vision, before I was able to make the leap to going for it fully.

Each new endeavor has taken me closer to what feels like the fullest expression of myself in the world. Some people may be blessed with knowing what their path is and go straight to it without much deviation. For others it may be a gradual progression. There is no one way to make the transition to work that is fulfilling and expresses who you are, though more than likely you will find many of the suggestions in this book useful in helping you along the way.

Pitfalls to Manifesting Your Dreams

The following are pitfalls you may face in manifesting a career change or dream. Notice whether you are holding some of the beliefs and attitudes mentioned here; then work with yourself using the tools discussed in this book. In doing this you can face the feelings associated with limiting attitudes and transform the paralyzing effects they create on your ability to pursue right livelihood.

Negative traps to watch out for:
Putting a lot of attention on why your dream can't be achieved
"Too many other people are doing it."
"I'm not good or experienced enough, or others are so much better at it than me."
"It will take too long to get going."
"There is too much competition."

Lack of strong intention or willingness to do what ever it takes
Even if you don't know the exact end result, if you have a strong desire and intention to move in a particular direction, miracles can happen, doors will open, opportunities may arise, or people will appear to help. Willingness and strong intention can help carry you through all the unknowns and give you the energy to follow through on what you wish to do. Many people never actively seek change but rather believe that some day, magically, their "ship will come in." Due to lack of intention, many people never start or persevere.

Lacking persistence or ability to hold the long range vision
If you have the willingness to start but don't have the ability to

persist, you will not be prepared to deal with the challenges that invariably arise. You may resort to telling yourself all the reasons why it can't be done, then quit rather than use the challenges as fuel to fire your determination. If you have already put a lot of energy out, it is good to periodically rest a bit to integrate what you have already put out, then wait for the spirit to move you before you begin fully again. This can help prevent burnout and give you a second wind.

Waiting for everything to be perfect before starting
Not moving until you have complete information, all the money you need, and approval or support from all those close to you (or others), will surely stop you from manifesting your dreams. You don't have to know exactly where you are going to get started; having a strong sense of what you want is enough. Getting started often helps build momentum that will clarify your vision.

Believing that it's not OK to change your mind
Not starting for fear of doing the wrong thing is more likely to lead to the wrong thing than not starting at all. It is often necessary to start moving down path A to get enough energy going to manifest path B or C, which could be the more appropriate path for you. If your intuition or circumstances are telling you Path A is not it, and you continue on A only because you believe it's not OK to change your mind or feel you will have wasted time, energy, or money, then it is a true waste of time. However, often path A is a necessary stepping stone to where you are going, providing either the training you need or useful connections.

Using excessiveness as a shield
Excessiveness means filling your life with so much that you can't experience having enough. This leaves little room left for exactly what you do want or for the simplicity that supports focus. It is biting off more than you can chew so that you can't accomplish anything. It is being so busy that nothing gets accomplished in a focused way—mistaking move-

ment for true action. In working with this issue it is helpful to look at your core beliefs to discover if one implies, "I am not enough or there is not enough." When this is the case not only do we tend to over fill our lives with too much to do but we also tend to collect a lot of material "stuff."

Being overwhelmed by the vision

Remember, achieving a dream is a marathon, not a sprint. If the vision seems too big, you can use stepping stones along the way. Aim for the ledge just ahead of you while holding the vision of the mountain top. Let your focus be on what is before you and do-able so you can accomplish plenty of wins and successful learning experiences. Remember there is no such thing as a failure, just an opportunity for refinement. Define what success means for you, and if it seems impossible to attain, redefine it to something that will allow you continuous wins. For example, go from success equals a certain amount of money in the bank to success equals learning something useful.

Unwillingness to trust

This is being unwilling to trust yourself or your intuition, which makes you unwilling to take risks. It may also mean unwillingness to trust Spirit or the flow of life. Practicing letting go of control comes in here.

The more you trust and experience positive results, the more references you have for believing that life will support you, and even take you where you're going. This gives you the courage to take risks, which is essential to manifesting miracles.

Pursuing right livelihood often requires working with many of the tools in this book: knowing your truth, being willing to express it, standing in that truth, taking risks, feeling the feelings that come up along the way and working through negative beliefs. It is not always quick and easy to make such a transition, but if you commit yourself to this path, it is inevitable that over time you will have more ability to passionately express yourself in life and through your work.

TRY IT!

Discovering Right Livelihood

1 | What do I love and what do I have to offer?

To discover where your heart and soul would thrive and where you could most fully express your unique and creative self in the world, answer the following questions (Credit to Global Family for this series of questions)[18]:

❑ What gifts have I been given to use, either natural talents I came in with or those that I have been blessed to have acquired in this life?

❑ What do I love to do?

❑ What gives me great satisfaction?

❑ Have I ever done anything that felt like I was making a contribution? What was it?

❑ When have I felt totally successful and joyful? What was I doing?

❑ What worked for me then that I could use in other aspects of my life now?

❑ What am I really good at?

❑ When have I been able to sustain a high level of performance with a high level of personal energy? What are the characteristics of these times: the work, the people, the physical environment, and the results?

❑ If money were no object, what would I be doing with my days?

❑ If all the conditions were right (family, education, time) what would I be doing with my life?

❑ What do I feel really passionate about?

❑ If I had only one year to live, what would I do?

Sit with your answers for awhile and let ideas for what you could do "bubble up." Do not judge the ideas as too difficult, too expensive, too many others doing it, or otherwise not do-able. You are *brainstorming*—letting creative ideas flow—which must be done without judgment.

If you don't get many ideas at first, keep the answers to these questions in mind for a longer period and eventually something will pop up that feels good. The next questions will also help you with this. It is best to have first worked with other exercises in this book so that underlying beliefs and emotions don't sabotage your good intentions.

2 | What do I not want?

If you have too much resistance to being straightforward about what you want, try this back-door approach, laid out by Barbara Sher.[19]

❑ "What would be the worst possible job I could think of?" Include the types of people involved, hours, location, environment, what you would be doing or not doing, pay—as many details as you can think of.

❑ "What do I dislike most about the job I do now or jobs I have done in the past?" Be specific.

❑ List the specifics of the your ideal job based on the opposite characteristics you described above. Do not worry about being practical by thinking of job possibilities you already know about. Just describe the qualities and details that counterbalance what you specifically dislike.

3 | Grounding intention

Integrating the answers from the previous questions, answer the following:

❏ "What am I here to do?"

❏ "If I knew I could not fail, what would I do?"

❏ "What are possible livelihood options through which these things (answers to previous questions) can express?"

❏ "What are the first steps (either small or large) I can take to move in this direction?"

❏ "What is my long-range game plan for moving in this direction?"

4 | Holding the Question

In addition to answering this series of questions, hold the question, that is, repeat daily as a prayer saying, "How can I best serve?" or "What are my best gifts, and how can I bring them forth to serve in the world?"

conclusion

The Journey Begins

Now it is time to continue your journey by yourself. Are you willing to do the work: to face and honor truth, to tell your truth, and be fully present, honest, and authentic with yourself and others in each moment, regardless of the apparent consequences? Will you accept this challenge, however scary it may seem? Can you look another in the eyes without wavering, being willing to be seen in your raw nakedness, for all that you have done or haven't done, for all that you are, are not, or could be? Are you willing to love and accept yourself no matter what?

How willing you are to face your own truth equals how willing you are to be seen and to express the truth of who you are. Anything less is a pretense, an adulteration of the truth, and won't help you express yourself to the fullest potential or truly make a difference to yourself or others. Giving from any other place is self-serving even when it appears to be noble. For if your heart really longs to serve, to make a difference and turn things around on this planet, you must start right here in the simple, quiet domain of your own backyard—in your own inner garden. For it is the garden of the soul that will bloom the flowers of your gifts that touch and heal the hearts of others.

Nothing brings more joy and happiness than when we are truly and honestly giving to others—not from our defectiveness but from our fullness, from a place that expresses who we are. True dedication to the journey will occasionally bring tears of sorrow and sadness but will also fill us with tears of joy. Embarking on this journey of truth, trust, expression, and creativity, though at times perhaps perilous, will lead to an adventurous, fun, creative, and fulfilling life.

About the Author

Joy Lynn Freeman, D.C., Ph.D. (candidate), has been a pioneer in the healing arts for over twenty years, as a natural physician, speaker-facilitator, body/mind therapist and personal coach. She has also produced a series of five health videos and co-created *Quantum Shift Retreats*—transformational retreats and workshops incorporating expressive arts, therapy, ritual, and nature.

Joy expresses her creativity as a singer, dancer and musician and through creative projects such as the music CD, *Let It Shine*, with lyrics that support the themes in *Express Yourself*. She is also currently conducting workshops and retreats on the awakening process. These workshops encourage people to creatively express themselves through voice, dance, rhythm and various forms of improvisation and opens them to their deeper truth, creative self, and a more expressive life.

To share your journey with Joy, contact her by writing to:
    PO Box 21266
    Boulder, CO 80308-4266,
or through her web site at www.SoundStarProductions.com.

notes

1 Hendrix, Harville. *Keeping the Love You Find*. New York: Pocket, 1992.

2 Chopra, Deepak, *The Path to Love*. New York: Three Rivers Press, 1997.

3 Frankl, Viktor E. *Man's Search for Meaning*. New York: Simon & Schuster, 1984.

4 Gray, John. *What You Can Feel, You Can Heal*. Mill Valley, CA: Heart Publishing, 1984, 12-17.

5 Glasser, William. *Control Theory*. New York: Harper Collins, 1985.

6 Cameron, Julia. *The Artist's Way,* New York: G. P. Putnam's Sons, 1992.

7 Hendricks, Gay & Kathlyn. *Conscious Relationship Training Manual*. Santa Barbara: The Hendricks Institute, Inc., 1993.

8 Branden, Nathaniel. *Experience High Self Esteem*. Audio Tape Series. New York: Pocket, 1988.

9 Hendricks, Gay & Kathlyn. *Body-Centered Therapy Training Manual*. Santa Barbara: The Hendricks Institute, Inc., 1993.

10 Laskow, Leonard. *Healing With Love*. Mill Valley: Wholeness Press, 1998.

11 Tart, Charles. *States of Consciousness*. New York: Dutton, 1975.

12 Gagan, Jeannette M. *Journeying: Where Shamanism and Psychology Meet*. Santa Fe: Rio Chama, 1998.

13 Katz, Irv. Unpublished manuscript. Carlsbad, CA.

14 Robbins, Anthony. *Awaken the Giant Within,* New York: Fireside, 1992.

15 Robbins, Anthony. Seminars and Trainings.

16 Jampolsky, Jerry. *Love Is Letting Go of Fear*. Berkeley: Celestial Arts, 1979.

17 Murry, W., from the Scottish Himalayan Expedition.

18 Treadgold, Rich, Marion Culhane & Carolyn Anderson of Global Family. San Anselmo, CA: Core Group Process, 1988.

19 Sher, Barbara. *I Could Do Anything If I Only Knew What It Was*. New York: Dell, 1994.

Recommended reading

Arrien, Angeles. *The Four-Fold Way*. San Francisco: Harper, 1993.

Blanton, Brad. *Radical Honesty*. New York: Dell, 1996.

Briggs, Dorthy C. *Celebrate Your Self*. New York: Doubleday, 1977.

Branden, Nathaniel. *Experience High Self Esteem*. Audio Tape Series. New York: Pocket, 1988.

Cameron, Julia. *The Artist's Way,* New York: G. P. Putnam's Sons, 1992.

Cohen, Alan. *Lifestyles of the Rich in Spirit*. Carlsbad, CA: Hay House, Inc., 1996.

Cohen, Alan. *The Dragon Doesn't Live Here Anymore*. Somerset, NJ: Alan Cohen Publications, 1990.

Derman, Bruce. *We'd Have a Great Relationship If it Weren't for You*. Deerfield Beach, FL : Health Comm, Inc., 1994.

Faber, Adele & Elaine Maxlish. *How To Talk So Kids Will Listen & Listen So Kids Will Talk*. New York: Avon, 1980.

Gagan, Jeanette M. *Journeying: Where Shamanism and Psychology Meet*. Santa Fe: Rio Chama, 1998.

Global Family. *Rings of Empowerment and Connecting at the Heart: A Global Family Guide to the Core Group Process*. 112 Jordan Avenue, San Anselmo, CA 94960.

Gray, John. *What You Can Feel, You Can Heal*. Mill Valley, CA: Heart Publishing, 1984.

Hay, Louise L. *You Can Heal Your Life*. Santa Monica: Hay House, 1984.

Hendricks, Gay & Kathlyn. *Conscious Loving*. New York: Bantam, 1990.

Hendricks, Gay. *Learning to Love Yourself*. New York: Prentice Hall, 1987.

Hendrix, Harville. *Keeping the Love You Find*. New York; Pocket, 1992.

Ingerman, Sandra. *Soul Retrieval: Mending the Fragmented Self*. San Francisco: Harper, 1991.

Jampolsky, Gerald G. *Love Is Letting Go of Fear*. Berkeley: Celestial Arts, 1979.

Laskow, Leonard. *Healing With Love*. Mill Valley: Wholeness Press, 1998.

Pierrakos, Eva. *The Pathwork of Self-Transformation*. New York; Bantam, 1990.

Pollard, John R. *Self Parenting*. Malibu, CA: Generic Human Studies Publishing, 1987.

Robbins, Anthony. *Awaken the Giant Within*. New York: Fireside, 1992.

Sher, Barbara. *I Could Do Anything If I Only Knew What it Was*. New York: Dell, 1994.

Stone, Hal & Sidra Stone. *Embracing Your Inner Critic*: Turning Self-Criticism into a Creative Asset. San Francisco: Harper, 1993.

Video Tapes by Joy Lynn Freeman

Videos

(Under the name Dr. L. J. Nelson)

Back-care-cise Videos

Prevent and relieve back pain while energizing your whole body.

Tape A—Gentle exercises that will strengthen and stretch your whole spine and mainly focuses on the lower back.

Tape B—Increased strengthening and stretching for the upper and lower back.

Tape C—Total body stretch and tone once you have mastered Tapes A and B.

Neck and Upper Back—Specific exercises to free the neck and upper back.

Shoulder, Wrist and Elbow—Prevent or relieve pain in the upper extremities

Dr. Nelson (Freeman) simply and gently teaches you precise and safe movements to:

✦ Eliminate back, neck or shoulder pain
✦ Strengthen and tone weak back muscles
✦ Increase flexibility and improve posture
✦ Relieve stress and boost energy

Tapes A, B, C, or Neck	$24.95 each or 3 for $59.95
Shoulder Video	$29.95
Shipping & Handling	$5.00 first video, $.60 each additional
	Quantity discounts available

To order call
800-736-2791

Other Products by Joy Lynn Freeman

BOOK & CD

Express Yourself(Book)	$12.95	+$5.00 S&H
Let It Shine(Music CD)	$15.95	+$4.00 S&H
(Cassette)	$10.00	+$4.00 S&H
Together as a set(Book & CD)	$22.95	+$5.50 S&H

Quantity Discounts Available

"Let It Shine" music CD is a unique blend of rhythmic and melodic flavors from smooth jazz, R&B, gospel, and world beat. It is contemporary music with a positive message. The songs, which are sung by a variety of soulful vocal artists, touch on themes which are expanded upon the the book *Express Yourself*.

To order call
SoundStar Productions
800-932-2483

or visit our web site
www.SoundStarProductions.com

~ ~ ~

Call for more information on workshops, corporate trainings, private or corporate coaching, or to arrange an inspirational and interactive speaking/singing presentation.

Express Yourself Retreats

Group Vacations on Maui

Play in waterfalls off the beaten path, hike in the jungle, splash in the warm blue ocean and luxuriate on quiet beaches. Take a week off that will truly be the vacation of your life as you will not come back the same. Experience the transformation that occurs with immersing yourself in nature, expressing in creative ways and connecting with the essence of yourself and others.

Retreats include workshops, yoga, nature excursions, gourmet vegetarian meals, tropical accommodations, (sometimes held at other beautiful locations). Optional: private session with Joy, massage, therapeutic body work, boat trips, snorkeling, kayaking or other fun adventures.

Private Retreats

Individually designed and include:
✦ Daily private sessions with Joy Lynn Freeman,
✦ Nature excursions
✦ Yoga

Accommodations and meals vary
according to individual needs.

To schedule a workshop in your area or
for more details on retreats call:

800-932-2483
www.SoundStarProductions.com